Ponies

Ponies

Candida Geddes

Sundial

Contents

First published in Great Britain in 1978 by Sundial Publications Limited,
59 Grosvenor Street, London, W1

Second impression, 1979

© 1978 Hennerwood Publications Limited

ISBN 0 904230 57 0

Produced by Mandarin Publishers Limited, 22a Westlands Road,
Quarry Bay, Hong Kong

Printed in Hong Kong

The Story of the Pony

RIGHT A narrow, long-legged Lesotho pony of southern Africa. This is one of many regions of the world where ponies are used to help man with his work, and yet have to fend for themselves in the matter of finding food. Such animals are bred not for beauty but for survival and for usefulness in whatever man-made tasks they are asked to perform.

The history of man is inextricably bound up with that of the horse. One of the earliest animals to be domesticated, the horse has served man and been served by him for thousands of years. Horses have been worshipped, have conferred power and position on men and on gods, figure frequently in mythology, and have played a unique part in spreading civilization and in achieving conquest throughout the world. The distinction between a 'horse' and a 'pony' is a modern one; in ancient times no such distinction existed, and indeed most of the 'horses' in use in the ancient world were what today would be classified as ponies. In the context of history, therefore, the word 'horse' is generally used to mean all equids, and in this chapter we will also use the word to include both ponies and horses.

According to an ancient Greek legend, Poseidon, the god of the sea, created the horse; another declares that God created the horse by breathing on a handful of the south wind. The precise origins of the modern horse are not known. It is now generally agreed among experts, however, that the modern horse is derived from four primitive types. These have been classified. Pony Type I was a native of north-western Europe and the outlying islands, and was rather similar to the modern Exmoor pony. Pony Type II is believed to have migrated westwards from central Siberia. Larger than Type I, it was also coarser and heavier in build, with a stiff, upright mane; the Asiatic or Mongolian Wild Horse, now known by the name of the Russian explorer Colonel Nikolai Przewalski, who discovered it in 1881, most closely represents this type and is today bred in zoos. Horse Type III was indigenous to central Asia, and was the largest of the four types, narrow in build with a long back and long head. Horse Type IV, on the other hand, was a small, fine-boned, elegant animal with a concave profile to its head now regarded as typical of the Arabian; the Caspian pony gives the best example today of this type.

Anthony Dent, a distinguished historian of the horse, has further defined these types by the characteristics most important to their survival. He calls Type I 'waterproof' Type II 'frostproof', Type III 'droughtproof' and Type IV 'heatproof', in reference to the predominant climatic feature of the region in which each of these types evolved. The ability of each to prosper depended greatly on its ability to adapt to its existing environment and to the food available; climatic changes and, later, perhaps beneficial intervention by man began to improve their living conditions, and some of them were able to grow much larger. In their original state Types I, II and IV, which played the major part in the development of the ancestors of the horses and ponies of today, were all small, pony-sized animals.

These types did not each live in complete isolation, as the classification above might seem to suggest. The majority of ponies found throughout Europe, for example, originally descended from natural crosses between Type I and Type II; the heavy agricultural horses and those used for war in medieval Europe were the product of crosses between Type II and Type III, gradually increasing in size thanks to feeding and shelter provided by man; Types III and IV produced the light, 'oriental' horses, varying in size and in substance according to the different habitats in which they bred. The horse, in its various modern forms, was indigenous only to Europe and Asia; it spread throughout the other continents as a result of man's own movements of exploration and colonization across the globe.

The history of the world's single most important breed, the Arab, is difficult to establish. The sand and wind of the Arabian desert, which has always been its home, erases all traces of human and animal remains, and archaeology has thus been unable to throw much light upon the early history, human or equine, of this part of the world. Historians of the horse have had to interpret as best they could the legends of the bedouin peoples of the desert, who have treasured these horses in an association which extends back for thousands of years. The prophet Mohammed (6-7th century), realising the value of the horse, promised access to heaven for all those who bred and cared for their horses. The harsh environment native to the Arab horse undoubtedly

played a part in developing the unique properties of soundness of limb and wind, speed and stamina, as well as of beauty: the Arab is generally regarded as the most beautiful of all horses. It also has the ability (known as *prepotency*) to pass on its own characteristics to its descendants, and many other breeds have for hundreds, if not thousands, of years benefited from the introduction of Arab blood. It was also the Arab, crossed with native English mares, which produced the world's finest modern horse, the English Thoroughbred, which has in turn contributed to the improvement in quality in many other breeds of both horses and ponies in recent times.

Ponies and Man

Man's first acquaintance with the horse was as a source of food: he hunted it. The next stage was the domestication of the horse for food: milk and meat that was tethered or penned outside the door was more convenient than food which had to be searched for and hunted down. Pastoralists, men who grazed — and still graze — domestic animals without settling in one place, later discovered that they could use the horse to carry their bedding, cooking pots and other possessions as they moved with their animals in their continual search for pastures. From there it must have been only a short step to riding horses — a privilege possibly accorded first to the weakest members of the tribe rather than to the most important. Some of the earliest horsemen were probably those of northern Europe who had previously domesticated and ridden the reindeer.

When, some 7,000 years ago, men began to settle in one place and cultivate the land, horses became increasingly important in communications and trade between one settlement and another. The first true civilizations, which arose in the 'Fertile Crescent' of the Near East, between the Tigris and the Euphrates rivers, and in the Nile valley in Egypt, have all left remains which clearly indicate the importance of horses as a symbol of a man's wealth and power. The Assyrian kings had themselves depicted astride horses on reliefs decorating their palace walls; the Egyptians both rode horses for hunting and harnessed them to chariots. Horses, chariots and accoutrements have been found in the graves of kings along with other particularly treasured goods they might need in the next

ABOVE The autumn round-up of cattle in Arizona. The cowboy's equipment has evolved from that of the 16th-century Spanish colonists: the saddle is comfortable for both pony and rider on long, tiring drives; the bitless bridle gives excellent control when used sensitively on a properly trained pony.

LEFT Indians at the Calgary Stampede, Alberta. Although there were no horses in the New World until the European conquests in the 16th century, many of the native American tribes were quick to see their value. Eventually horses were to transform their methods of hunting and waging war.

ABOVE Another example of a rural community where ponies are still expected to help man earn his living: this pony is carrying away bags of grain after the harvest winnowing in rural Haiti.

RIGHT In mountainous areas, and other districts where the terrain is difficult, a pony is more useful to the farmer than a machine, and more versatile. This Fjord pony mare turning hay is 20 years old but still makes a contribution to the work of the farm.

world. That the Greeks valued horses is attested not only by the magnificent horses of the Parthenon but also on innumerable vases and other pieces of painted pottery. One of the most important men in the history of any age, Alexander the Great, had a horse so famous that its name has survived: Bucephalus, the steed which, according to popular legend, would permit only Alexander himself to ride it. Bucephalus carried Alexander at the head of his armies from Macedon (in what is now northern Greece) through Asia Minor, Persia and Afghanistan to the foothills of the Hindu Kush mountains, and then into the valley of the Indus river, where the city of Bucephala was founded and named in its honour.

Recorded history still does not distinguish between horses and ponies, although it is assumed that monarchs and other important leaders were mounted on the best and largest available animals. Ponies, however, were undoubtedly used in all the lands in which they flourished, and they gave their riders superiority over a man on foot. The legend of the centaurs is thought to have originated in some 'horseless' region, in response to what must have been the terrifying sight of a man mounted on a pony, his legs hidden by the animal's shaggy coat

so that he appeared to be a part of the animal, not a separate being.

Perhaps the first example of a distinction being made between the pony and the horse is to be found in the reign of the Chinese emperor Wu-ti of the Han dynasty. In 128 BC one of his ambassadors reported the fine horses he had seen in the region around Samarkand, in Uzbekistan. Some years later Wu-ti sent a special expedition to obtain some of these animals; they became known as the 'heavenly horses', and were regarded as greatly superior both in stature and in power to the small, pony-type steppe horses native to China, which would have resembled the stolid Przewalski. There are numerous examples in Chinese art of these superior horses; indeed, horses figure so largely in the art of different epochs of ancient Chinese history that it is clear they were as treasured in this part of the world as they were in Europe and western Asia.

Much of the history of Eurasia has been punctuated by the devastating effects of hordes of nomadic barbarians on agricultural civilizations: Huns, Vandals, and Goths destroyed the Roman Empire in the west; later, Magyars, Vikings, and Saracens plundered, raided, and eventually settled. One of the most important of these incursions was the Mongol invasions of the 13th and 14th centuries, particularly under their two greatest leaders, Genghis Khan and Timur the Lame (Tamerlane). Their armies overran most of Asia and Europe, from Peking to the gates of Vienna, irrupting out of the steppes in wave upon wave of archers riding Mongolian ponies of incredible toughness. That the Mongols knew how much their success depended upon their ponies cannot

be doubted; their conquests were planned to allow for travel and rest periods before battles, and the womenfolk were employed looking after the spare ponies of each warrior.

Another outstanding example of the effect mounted men can have is that of the arrival of the Spanish *conquistador* Hernando Cortes in Mexico in 1518. He took 11 stallions and 5 mares with him to a continent whose inhabitants had never seen a horse of any kind. The effect was overwhelming; as Cortes himself said, 'After God, we owed our victory to the horses.' Although it is possible that there were primitive horses native to the Americas about 20,000 years ago, when there was a 'land-bridge' between Asia and America across Bering Strait, there were certainly none when Cortes arrived. Some of the horses taken by him and his successors escaped, and the native horse population was thus introduced.

In their turn, the native horses of America were to have a profound effect upon the exploration and settlement of the continent by the white man. Even if Western films are exaggerated, where would the American cowboy have been without his pony? On the huge ranches of the United States, cow ponies are still invaluable as working members of every herding team. They provide, too, a further example of the confusion between 'horse' and 'pony': cow ponies are always known as such, and yet they are descended from horses, not from ponies. In South America the *gauchos* of Argentina ride 'ponies', and indeed have bred polo 'ponies' from them with great success. And the most famous, perhaps, of any Wild West legend is that of the Pony Express, whose riders carried the mail across dangerous country from St Joseph, Missouri to Sacramento in California in 1860 and 1861. Their mounts, too, were descended from horse ancestors, but in the intervening years these had lost height and substance through living in the wild. The Indians by whom they were attacked were also mounted. Although at first they had been frightened of the horse, Indians quickly realised that they could take advantage of the example set them by the white man, and became excellent horsemen — even though they were generally careless horsemasters.

It is true to say that, until the development of the railways and the invention of the internal-combustion engine in the 19th century, almost every significant civilization the world has known has depended on the horse for its transport, the

ABOVE This is one of the ways the westward-pushing European colonizers explored America: with ponies to ride, and ponies and mules carrying packs of equipment and supplies. The modern sport of trail riding keeps alive the traditions of this method of travel.

11

success of its armies, the status of its kings, the pursuit of trade, and the diffusion of culture and knowledge. If there had been no horses, the history of the world would have been vastly different.

Ponies are still used, as are horses, in many parts of the world in a working role. Only in the industrialized countries are they used almost exclusively for pleasure — and even there one might argue that, from the point of view of the pony, it is still work. It is only very recently, too, that ponies have come to be regarded as suitable mounts for children. Throughout their history, ponies have been ridden by adults whose weight they have borne patiently and without undue discomfort; they are not, however, asked to perform at a gallop or to jump artificial fences when they are playing their part in agriculture and industry. There are many countries where ponies have a vital traditional role; and in other circumstances new tasks are being found for them by men looking for new ways to earn a living. All over the world, for thousands of years, native ponies have been used by farmers and well-to-do peasants in almost every aspect of their daily work. For ploughing heavy land, horses are required; but for many other farming activities sturdy ponies are the most versatile assistants. They can cover greater distances than a man on foot, and increase his horizons: for herding sheep and cattle, and for the inspection of boundary fences on huge grazing ranges, for example, they save the farmer's time and energy. They can carry a heavy load and surefootedly pick their way down a mountainside at the same time; they are hardy and healthy, generally surviving on little fodder and with little care; docile and reliable, they are more even-tempered than a mule and more versatile than a donkey. Ponies were used for packwork for thousands of years all over northern Europe, for neither the ass nor the mule was known north of the Alps until the beginning of the Christian era; indeed, until much more recently, strings of pack ponies were a familiar sight in the dales of northern England, carrying lead from the mines to the ports for shipment abroad.

Modern Working Ponies

Even in western Europe and North America, deliveries of merchandise and transport of people relied entirely on ponies and horses until well into the present century. Indeed, until only a few years ago milk floats were drawn by ponies even in London, and a pony which knew its round would stop at the right houses without having to be told. Coster ponies are still a familiar sight, as are the ponies of the totters, as cockney rag-and-bone men are called. In many towns in the less-developed parts of the world a pony and cart is still regarded as the normal way to travel, and in country districts it remains

FAR LEFT ABOVE *Cabyard at Night,* an evocative scene painted by Robert Bevan in 1910, recalls the days before the internal-combustion engine made horses and ponies virtually redundant in cities throughout the industrialized world.

FAR LEFT BELOW A sprightly pony trots briskly along a hilly road in County Kerry, south-western Ireland. The pony is obviously well cared for, even though its equipment seems to be a little makeshift.

LEFT Wherever ponies form part of the local scene they will be found in parades and festivals. Suitably decked out for the occasion, this pony is ready to take part in the Sliema Festival in Malta.

the *only* way to travel except on foot. Civilization in the form of mechanization has been slow to reach all corners of the globe, and in many regions its use in transport is either uneconomic or impossible. A machine cannot acquire 'cow sense' in the rounding up of cattle, and ponies go lame less often than machines break down. Nor can a machine work in mountainous areas, or in thick forests, where ponies are still found — in Scandinavia and in Germany, for example — helping to drag fallen tree trunks to the forest roads for transport to the timber mills.

Tourism has provided a new field of activity for ponies all over the world. Beach ponies have been a familiar sight for a long time, as Victorian photograph albums demonstrate. Nowadays, one may be driven over the snow of Switzerland or Austria, through the lush vegetation of an Indonesian island, or past the classical splendours of Greece, or the pyramids of Egypt, in gaudily painted traps pulled by seemingly tireless ponies. It seems that the farther industrial man moves away from animals in his working day, the greater is their appeal for him in his leisure time. Ponies have been a popular feature for many years in that ancient, enduring form of entertainment, the circus. While welfare societies point out the cruelty of caging wild animals for use in circuses, the pony acts —

which are so obviously enjoyed by the performers — become increasingly welcome. Highly trained and skilful, and displaying uncanny adroitness and sense of timing, these ponies demonstrate the closeness of the bond that can develop between them and their trainers.

Another important new task for ponies has given benefit to thousands of deprived humans: the physically or mentally handicapped. The Riding for the Disabled movement, which began in Scandinavia and has now spread rapidly to countries all over the world, has proved a tremendous success in extending the limited world of those with severe disabilities. Children who have been confined to a wheelchair acquire a new freedom of movement and a new feeling of independence by riding, and take particular delight in it. The ponies are specially picked for their steadiness and utter reliability; they and the volunteer helpers who guide them provide a valuable form of therapy and give tremendous pleasure at the same time.

This is just one function of ponies in riding schools, of which there has been a tremendous increase in recent years. Ponies have been given a new dimension in their relationship with man, and they have ensured their future just at the time when it seemed that they would soon outlive their usefulness. In the following pages we take a look at the modern pony and his world.

PAGES 14-5 At the Nadom Festival at Hujirt, in the high plains of the northern Hangay region of Mongolia, horsemen create a scene straight out of history. Their Mongol forebears of the vast central Asian steppes, who conquered so much of the Eurasian landmass, cannot have looked very different.

Know Your Ponies

All ponies and horses belong to the same species, *Equus caballus*. This may seem surprising when we think of the great variations in size and shape between, say, a massive Clydesdale draught horse, a sleek Derby winner, and a diminutive pit pony. The fact is, however, that all such variations are accounted for by differences in breed and type. What do these two terms mean?

Modern pony *breeds* are descended from wild herds that evolved certain physical characteristics as a result of settling permanently in particular kinds of habitat. The elements in the environment that influenced evolutionary development include climate, the nature of the terrain, the nature and availability of food, the other animals with which the ponies had to compete for food, and the presence or absence of natural enemies. In each generation the weeding-out process called natural selection would have favoured, within each herd, those individuals best fitted for survival in their specific habitat. And so, over countless generations, the herds would have tended to be made up of ponies of much the same size, shape, and other physical qualities. In other words, they evolved particular characteristics that distinguished them from ponies living in other kinds of habitat — characteristics that have endured and have enabled us to define them as a breed.

Today pony breeds are the subject of carefully compiled records (stud books) kept by various breed societies. Only pure-bred ponies can be registered with the societies, and breeding from these animals is strictly regulated to ensure that the purity of the blood-lines is maintained and the physical characteristics that define each breed are perpetuated.

The term *type* cuts across blood-lines. A pony can be described as being of a particular type only if it has the combination of certain physical characteristics (which may include colouring) formally recognized as defining that type. A number of types have arisen out of man's quest for various useful qualities in his ponies — strength, stamina, speed, surefootedness, docility, or whatever — irrespective of breed. A type may have its origin, then, in the deliberate mating of a mare and a stallion of different breeds. The resulting foals, however, will be recognized as constituting a type only if the characteristics that they inherited from their parents persist in subsequent generations by further cross-breeding.

Judging Pony Quality

Before considering the various breeds and types of pony we need to understand some of the methods by which they are judged and the terms used to describe their good and bad qualities. Five basic characteristics are involved: size, conformation, temperament, colour, and markings.

Horses and ponies are both measured in *hands:* a hand measures 10.2 cm (4 inches), which is regarded as the average span of a man's hand; this way of measuring is being maintained in spite of metrication. Ponies are measured from the ground to the withers (the bump where the neck joins the top of the back), and fractions of hands are given in inches. Thus a 12.2 hands (or h.h. — hands high) pony is 127 cm (50 inches) in height. Height plays a part in pony competitions, because height limits divide various classes both in showing and in jumping events.

Conformation is perhaps the most important ingredient in judging any pony for any purpose. The word means 'make and shape', and refers to a pony's looks and the way its body is put together. This matters not only for a show pony, whose success in the ring will depend largely on how beautiful an appearance it has, but for ponies of all kinds. A pony with good conformation is less likely to suffer from strains and lamenesses, and is more likely to be comfortable to ride — or will be better able to pull a cart or a plough — than one whose conformation is less good. The beauty of a top-class show pony is not only in its plaited mane and highly polished coat, but also in the *total* effect of its physical appearance.

To understand the difference between good and bad conformation requires much experience and study, as well as what experts call an 'eye' for what is right. Some

ABOVE The sturdy Døle pony of Norway, sometimes known as the Gudbrandsdal, has for centuries been used for pack work, and in both looks and character is similar to the Dales and Fell ponies of England. The trot is its best pace, and Døle ponies have been used widely in the breeding of Norwegian trotters for racing.

short, puddling sort of stride because it tends to prevent the pony from moving its forelegs freely. Free movement is essential in a pony if it is going to be comfortable to ride and will not tire easily, and a shoulder which slopes upwards from chest to withers is a good sign. The chest, viewed from the front, should be reasonably broad: if the forelegs seem to 'come out of one hole', as the expression is, there may be less than adequate room for the lungs and heart. A pony with long legs will probably have a longer stride than one with short legs; but generalization is difficult about the right length of leg because nature has endowed some breeds — the Shetland, for example — with extremely short ones. A relatively long-legged pony is likely to be able to gallop better than a stocky one. Whatever their length, the legs should be strong and well shaped, with a fair strength in the bone, and the all-important foot should be neither too square and 'boxy' nor too long-toed. The legs should stand straight, and in movement turn neither out nor in; the forelegs should not be 'pigeon-toed' (turning inwards), nor the hind legs 'cow-hocked' (hocks turning in towards each other, and feet correspondingly angled outwards). The pony's body should be fairly short in the back, as a long back is often a sign of weakness, and should be well rounded (this refers to the structure of the rib cage rather than the rotundity caused by the amount of surplus flesh a pony may carry), giving enough room, again, for the internal organs. The quarters should be strong, and not slope too much away towards the tail. Overall, a pony should look harmoniously in proportion with itself.

of the basic characteristics can, however, be described. The head is one of the important indicators of a pony's quality. It should seem small, rather than large, in proportion to the body; the ears should be short and alert, rather than long and slack; the eyes should be bright and intelligent, with no white showing. There is an almost indefinable quality known as 'ponyness', a mixture of intelligence and what in humans we would call mischief and humour, shrewdness and curiosity, which is an important characteristic in a pony — but it is an air rather than an obvious physical attribute, and it eludes description. The pony's head should be 'well set on' to the neck, at an angle which seems right and comfortable. The neck itself should be neither weedy and thin nor thick and stocky. Most ponies have a thickish mane and tail to give them warmth and protection from the weather; those with Arab or Thoroughbred blood will carry finer, silkier hair both in the mane and tail and in the coat.

The shoulder is another important indicator of the likely quality of a pony. A very straight shoulder may be acceptable for a pony that is to be driven rather than ridden. But in a riding pony it is likely to indicate a

Long and learned books are devoted to the subject of conformation, so this description cannot adequately describe all to look for. A standardized description of a well-made pony also cannot take into account the variations between the different breeds; but fundamentally the essentials of good conformation hold good for all ponies, and for horses too. The only way to assess conformation adequately is to look at ponies carefully, especially in the show ring. Riding them will also tell one a good deal about them: a comfortable pony with an elastic stride is unlikely to be badly made, while a very short-striding one, jerky in movement, is likely to be uncomfortable as well as less good to look at. Some faults of conformation can be corrected through careful schooling: for example, a weak 'ewe' neck, thin and lacking in muscle, can be immeasurably improved with training to build up the muscles on the top of the neck; but other faults are incurable. Knowing how a pony should look helps in assessing the chances of a particular pony being able to give a good performance — which a pony with chronically poor conformation will never be able to do, however well trained and willing it may be.

ABOVE There are two types of Highland pony: the large mainland type and the much smaller island type; both types are sturdy, docile, reliable, and much valued for their strength. These ponies are from the Isle of Rum.

RIGHT A well-trained Shetland pony makes an ideal first mount for a small child. This pony and its rider are confident in each other. Riding bareback will help her to develop a good seat, and she has clearly lost any early feelings of precariousness at riding without a saddle.

and grey are the only permitted colours for the breed. The same colour limitations apply to the Fell, which is slightly smaller at a maximum of 14 hands but is full of strength and endurance. Its stamina makes it a popular choice for the demanding sport of long-distance riding and, when cross-bred, for eventing.

Scotland's breeds, the Highlands and the Shetland, have also traditionally been used to help farmers with their work, and some of them still do. The Highlands pony has two types: those from the mainland, which are the larger at about 14.2 hands, and their island cousins which may be as little as 12.2 hands. Both strains are remarkably strong, agile, and surefooted; the commonest colour for the Highland is one of the shades of dun, usually with a dorsal stripe, but greys, bays, dark browns, and occasionally chestnuts are also found.

The Shetland is the only native breed which may be odd-coloured — piebald or skewbald — as well as any of the whole colours. It is the smallest of the native breeds (sometimes a mere 10 hands), but for its size it is the strongest. The hostile climate of its native islands has resulted in

the breed developing particularly abundant mane and tail hair as well as an extra-thick coat. Although the Shetland has become famous as a family pet, it too has for centuries been a working pony in the islands. Its size makes the Shetland a popular first pony, but its reputation has sometimes suffered as a result of it being treated too much as a pet; in fact it needs discipline, and its headstrong temperament may make it disobedient unless it is firmly handled.

The Connemara comes from the district of Galway, in the west of Ireland, from which it derives its name. The breed is an old one — hardy, surefooted, and able in its wild state to thrive on very little food. Connemaras, which may be up to 14 hands and are generally dun-coloured or grey, are used both for farm work and as riding ponies; their natural jumping ability makes them a popular choice among children.

A new type — not a breed — of pony has been developed in recent years, partly in response to the enormous increase of interest in show ponies. This is the English riding pony, which may be a cross of any of the native breeds with a small Thoroughbred or Arab sire. The best crosses produce superb ponies, retaining all the

ABOVE Norwegian ponies are one of the old northern European breeds, and are able to withstand extremely severe weather thanks to their thick coats. They have the stiff, upright mane found also in the primitive Przewalski, or Mongolian Wild Horse.

ABOVE The Huçul pony, bred traditionally in Poland (where these ponies were photographed), Romania, Czechoslovakia, and Austria, is a native of the Carpathian Mountains. Willing and strong, these ponies are excellent for pack and draught work.

hardiness, stamina and pony quality of the native breeds but with added refinement. These ponies are now bred all over the world, and studs have been set up to breed both the native ponies and the riding ponies from them as the demand for quality ponies has risen. The foundation stock for all these studs is drawn from the top studs in Britain.

Britain does not by any means have a monopoly of riding pony types and breeds. Many countries have native breeds of their own, but in general it is true to say that not one of these has proved internationally as popular or as versatile as its British counterparts. It is only relatively recently that the pony has come to be regarded as a suitable mount for children — or indeed for anyone who rides simply for pleasure. In every country where native ponies have bred in the wild — in Iceland, Timor, India,

and Greece, to give just a sample — they have been (and still are being) used as working ponies, for farm and pack transport, for shepherding and helping with the harvest, and for many other rural activities. Conversely, in parts of the world without native pony breeds, children have been expected to ride horses from an early age; in Australia and North America, for instance, one may see quite small children perched confidently upon horses. In recent years, however, and especially in America, a new interest in ponies has led to development of new breeds, of which two examples are the American Shetland, an elegant pony bearing little resemblance to its Scottish namesake, and the Pony of the Americas. Nevertheless, it is clear that the particular climate and environment in which the British ponies thrived for so many centuries without any help from man have combined to produce the world's outstanding pony breeds.

It is not necessary for a pony to be a pure-bred member of any breed for it to be a good pony. Thousands of foals of unknown pedigree are born every year, and most of them are just nice, ordinary ponies; their looks and their abilities vary, but even those with little chance of winning rosettes in the show ring may give a lifetime of pleasure to their riders.

Buying a pony can be rather like buying a house: there is a new language to learn, a confusion of experts to give advice, and a real delight if the right purchase is made. For those considering buying a pony, various decisions need to be made before a pony itself is sought. Who is likely to ride the pony: only small, light children, or a whole family eager to be mounted? Is there anybody in the family with experience in riding as well as in looking after ponies? If not, an absolutely safe, quiet pony will be more suitable than one which looks and performs like a champion but may not be quite so easy to handle. Anybody considering buying a pony for the first time should get expert help. The best place to seek this is from a riding-school instructor, from a Pony Club official, or from anybody who really knows about ponies but is a disinterested party. Most dealers are also honest, but they may sometimes be a little less careful than a personal acquaintance would be about matching a pony and a rider. The best possible way to buy a pony for a child is to buy one known to that child, perhaps one which has been outgrown by its present owner. The pony will have been seen in action, and the prospective buyer will know whether it is quiet and kind, or boisterous but a good performer.

Perhaps the two golden rules in buying a pony are, first, that the prospective owner should *like* the pony and the pony should seem, as far as it is possible to tell, to like its new rider; and, second, that the pony chosen should be suitable for the sort of riding that the new owner will want to do. A very quiet pony will make a boring mount for a capable and ambitious child; an energetic, strong pony will make an inexperienced, nervous child more nervous still, but may well bring out the best in a more determined and confident rider.

Ponies are sold through advertisements, through friends and dealers, and at auctions and fairs. These last two are strictly the province of the expert; buying a pony 'on spec' at an auction is unlikely to be a successful venture for the novice buyer. An honest dealer, preferably one who has been personally recommended and who specializes in ponies rather than horses, will do his best to find a suitable pony as long as the buyer gives him clear and sensible instructions as to the type of animal

required. But he will be unable to provide the right pony — and at the right price — if he is given a false impression, by doting parents or friends, of a child's ability and experience.

A pony that is to be bought through personal contact will almost certainly be allowed by its owner to go to its new home for a period 'on trial'. This arrangement relies on the goodwill of both parties, and should not be abused. The buyer either pays a deposit on the pony or pays for it in full on the understanding that if it proves unsuitable for any good reason it may be returned.

Pony Lingo
The language used in advertisements for ponies in the horse-world press is quite individual; and since these terms are also used in the riding world generally to

TOP An attractive Caspian pony stallion. The breed was thought to have been extinct for about 1,000 years until a few ponies were found in the area of the Caspian Sea in 1965. Recent research indicates that the Caspian is descended from the ancient breed of miniature horse.

ABOVE The ponies of Timor, an island in the Indonesian archipelago, are very small but so strong that they are used by the local 'cowboys' for rounding up cattle.

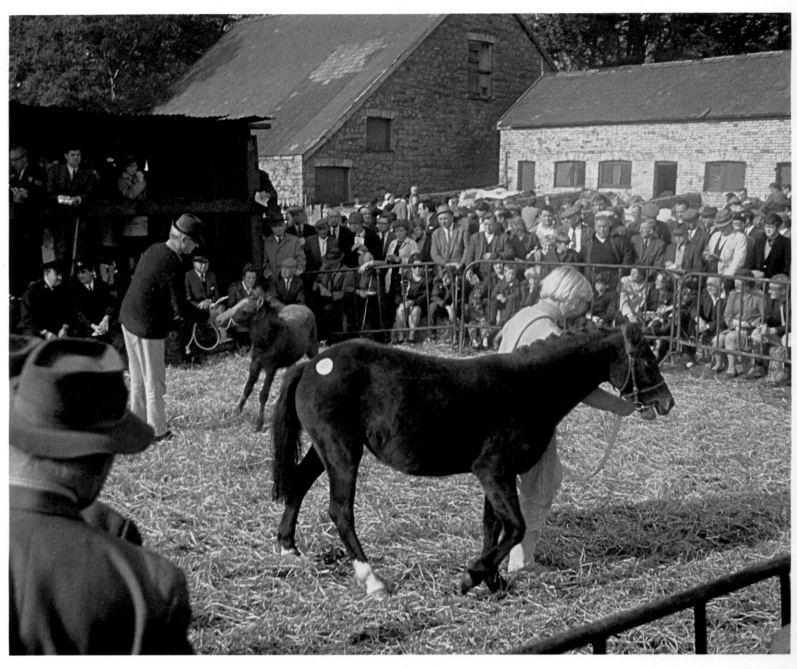

ABOVE A pony auction in
progress. Sales of native
breeds often draw large
crowds at local shows, but
bidding should be left strictly
to the expert buyer.

RIGHT One of the joys of
owning a pony is the
companionship which
develops between pony and
rider, but ownership is not
necessary for making friends,
either equine or human, with
whom one can explore the
countryside.

describe the degree of training and the
experience of a pony, it may be useful to
define some of them. *Breaking* or *breaking in*
a pony refers to its earliest, basic training:
learning to be handled, becoming accustomed to saddle and bridle, and to being
groomed and led; *backing* is the first stage of
getting a pony used to having a rider on its
back, usually at the age of four. A pony is
said to be *aged* when it is over eight years of
age. Up to that age the state of its teeth will
tell an expert how old it is; after that age
such evidence is less reliable. A four-year-
old pony which has been backed is regarded
as totally *green:* it still lacks both training
and experience, and would be an unsuitable
purchase for any but experienced pony-
owners. A pony's active life can be expected
to continue until it is well into its teens, and
many ponies live and work happily into
their twenties with good care. A *novice* pony
is one which has been schooled to a
reasonable standard but still lacks experience and would need a competent rider to
bring out its potential. A pony is said to be
made when its schooling is regarded as

sufficiently advanced for it to undertake the
work planned for it, and it has had some
experience. Even after this a pony's
schooling will need to be continued,
especially with a quality animal which may
be asked to compete in sporting events.
Ponies are said to be *honest* when they are
cooperative, have no tricks or nasty habits
beyond the occasional bout of high spirits,
and can be relied on to behave sensibly;
genuine means the same thing. Ponies
which are docile and responsible and so
suitable for an inexperienced child are
generally described as *first* ponies: they
should be absolutely quiet to handle, make
no fuss when having their feet picked up or
their saddlery put on, and submit willingly
to being groomed and played with. It must
be said that ponies are extremely receptive
to the ability and state of mind of the
handler: a pony which may behave perfectly
with one person may play all sorts of tricks
with another. Weakness or nervousness on
the part of the human is likely to be reflected
in disobedience in the pony; cruelty will
produce either fear or a violent response.

Pony Care

Looking after a pony is a different proposition from owning a pet cat or dog, and different again from the kind of care a farmer needs to give to cattle or sheep. It is more demanding than either. For anybody with a practical interest in ponies — even if that interest is limited to an occasional lesson at a riding school and a visit to the local gymkhana — it can only be an advantage to know about the varieties of equipment, the rudiments of schooling, and the care needed by different ponies in different conditions.

As we have already seen, ponies are herd animals, with a herd instinct still strong in them even though their ancestors may not actually have lived in a herd for generations. This instinct affects their reactions to many different things: to the stable or field which is their home, to their human owners, to other ponies they may meet or may live with, and so on. Most ponies are hardy enough not to require the full-time stabling which a Thoroughbred horse, for example, would need. But this does not mean that a pony which is expected to lead a working life can live happily and perform effectively on a diet of grass and with just an occasional visit from its owner.

Feeding

In the wild, ponies are able to sustain themselves adequately on the good grass provided by nature in the spring and early summer. They browse continuously, moving slowly with the herd. In winter they forage for what can be found, usually becoming thin and losing condition. The modern domesticated pony is expected to gallop (which the wild pony only does in short bursts to escape from danger) with a rider on its back, perhaps to jump and to take part in sports and rallies, or, in the case of a riding-school pony, to be ridden for several hours each day with different demands being made upon it by different riders. This very different kind of life requires a better, more balanced diet than grass if the pony is to keep in good condition. During the spring and early summer, when the grass is rich and full of nourishment, a pony can happily live out of doors. Too happily, in fact: the richness of grass grown with the help of modern fertilizers can tax a pony's constitution in various ways. A pony can become very fat on an excess of rich grass, and it may develop an excruciatingly painful disease of the feet known as laminitis; ponies that become excessively plump during the spring and summer have to be tied up or stabled without food for part of the day to ensure that they do not overeat.

In many circumstances ponies need supplementary feeding. Even a pony not in work will need a reasonable quantity of good quality bulk food such as meadow hay every day for much of the year, the quantity varying between about 2 and 5 kg (5 lb and 11 lb) depending on the weather, the condition of the grass when cut, and the size of the pony. A pony which is expected to work will, in addition to hay, need concentrates — high-energy, high-protein foods such as oats, maize, and bran. Ponies often do best on balanced concentrated foods, such as 'nuts' and 'cubes', which provide all the nourishment they need without being excessively 'heating' in the way that oats may be; nuts are also easier to store and to prepare than some other foodstuffs. In very cold weather even ponies not in work will need some concentrated food if they are not to lose condition.

The Paddock

A pony which is expected to live out all the year round and receives only modest quantities of supplementary food requires a paddock or field of between two and three acres. If the area available is less or the grazing poor, more supplementary feeding will be needed. Good grazing contains a high proportion of leafy grasses and clovers. The quality of a pony paddock is often improved by the presence of cattle, which eat the taller grasses that ponies tend to avoid and thus encourage the growth of the shorter grass species. Poisonous plants must be removed before a pony is turned out into a field: the most common include hemlock, ragwort, monkshood, green bracken, laurel, and yew. Buttercups are also a sign of poor pasture and are not good for ponies.

The paddock should be safely fenced to

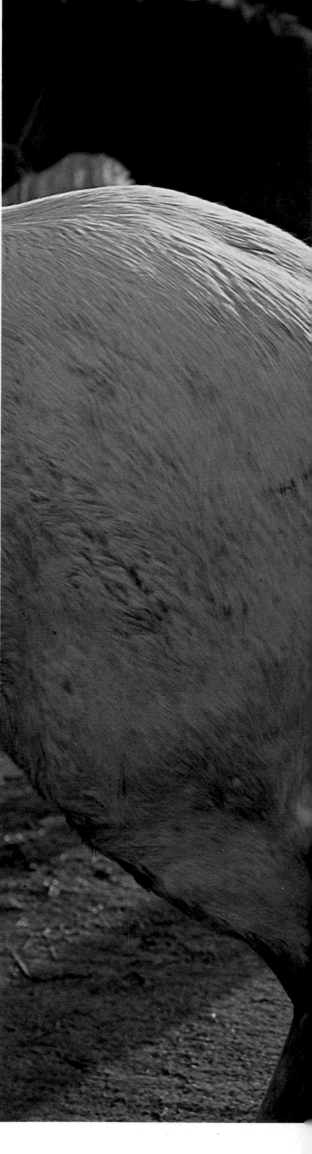

TOP Picking out the pony's feet is the most important part of the grooming routine for both grass-kept and stabled ponies. Note the triangular 'frog', which acts as a shock absorber, on the underside of the foot.

ABOVE When a pony's tail has been pulled it will keep its shape better if a tail bandage is put on when grooming has been completed.

RIGHT Brushing out a pony's tail greatly improves its appearance. It is generally advisable to stand to one side of the pony, rather than directly behind it as is being done here, in case it kicks.

ABOVE The basic item of tack (saddlery) needed for a pony: a saddle with girth, stirrup leathers, and irons, a bridle — in this case a snaffle (on wall) — and a headcollar and rope (at left on rug).

since grooming removes much of the natural grease that gives the coat its warmth, a pony permanently at grass should be much less vigorously groomed.

The first item in the grooming kit is the dandy brush, a stiff-bristled brush used to remove mud and dried sweat from the coat. It is fairly harsh, and therefore should not be used on tender, bony parts of the pony (such as its face), on the mane or tail (it will split the hairs), or on ponies with fine coats and sensitive skins. The body brush has shorter, softer bristles and is used to clean the coat of dust and grease; it is used in conjunction with a metal curry comb, which is used to clean the brush after every few strokes along the pony's coat. The curry comb itself is never used on the pony's coat. (Rubber curry combs have quite recently become popular, and they may be used on the pony's coat in order to remove stubborn sweat marks or patches of mud). The body brush is also used to brush out the mane and tail and to clean the pony's legs and face. The mane comb is used to undo tangles in the mane, and when 'pulling' mane or tail. A water brush is used to 'lay' the mane neatly along the neck, and to dampen the tail before putting on a tail bandage. The hoof pick is used to clean out the feet, in which mud, straw, stones, and other objects may lodge. This is perhaps the most important part of the cleaning routine, for infections and lameness can result from neglect of the feet. Two sponges are required: one to clean the eyes and nostrils, the other to clean the dock (under the tail) and genital area of the pony. A stable rubber (a linen cloth rather like a tea-towel) is used to give the coat a final polish. When a pony is being prepared to get into really 'hard', fit condition, a wisp is also used. It is made out of a twisted rope of hay, and is used to massage the muscles of the pony; a stable rubber bunched together can be used in the same way. This tones the muscles, as the wisp is brought down with some force onto the muscular areas of the pony's body; it should, however, be used with care because the pony will object violently — and may be injured — if it is banged on bony areas or on the loins.

The full grooming process should be carried out every day on a stabled pony, and also on ponies in work during the summer. For those out at grass, all that is needed is a quick brushing-over of the winter coat before going for a ride; the feet must be picked out, and brushing the mane and tail to remove tangles will make the pony look more presentable.

Coat, Mane, and Tail
The pony's coat must be dry when it is groomed — and one disadvantage of keeping a pony at grass is that it may be very wet and muddy when it is wanted for a ride. This is another reason for having a shelter into which the pony can be taken to dry out for an

its muscles slack, and its circulation sluggish. That pony, taken out of the field and asked to compete in a hunter trial with no preparation, will both perform badly and be considerably distressed. It needs a long period of slow, steady exercise and a gradual change in diet in order for it to become fit. The amount of exercise must take into account the exceptional activities which a pony will be asked to undergo. A pony leading an active life some of the time must be kept fit by regular exercise the rest of the time; a stabled pony needs a minimum of an hour's exercise every day, and preferably also some hours at liberty in a field.

Grooming is an essential part of conditioning a pony, but it is important to understand what grooming achieves and the right circumstances for it. A stabled pony must be thoroughly groomed every day. But a pony living outdoors needs the protection afforded by its thick coat; and

hour or two beforehand, so that it can be groomed and will not be wet and uncomfortable when ridden.

Ponies with very heavy coats fare well out of doors, but are never as fit as those with lighter ones. If a pony is to do a considerable amount of work, it is usually clipped during the winter. Clipping, which removes the long coat, is done with a clipping machine and should be carried out only by experts. For ponies, the most satisfactory clip is what is known as a trace clip, in which the underside of the neck and belly are clipped, extending to some little way up the flanks (about to the level of the harness traces), but the hair along the top of the pony's body is not touched. A trace-clipped pony is easier to keep clean, will dry more quickly after a wet ride, and is able to work harder and faster than a pony with a full coat. In cold weather the loss of warmth due to clipping needs to be compensated for, and even a trace-clipped pony will require rugs to keep it warm. In the stable a jute night rug is commonly used

ABOVE A farrier 'hot-shoeing' a pony. This method of shoeing causes no pain because the hoof wall to which the shoe is applied is insensitive tissue. Cold shoeing is, however, easier for a travelling farrier as he does not have to carry as much equipment, and he can make minor adjustments to a standard-sized shoe before nailing it to the foot.

NEAR RIGHT The saddle is placed gently over the pony's withers, a little farther forward than its final position so that it can be pushed to the rear, ensuring that the hairs lie flat underneath it.

MIDDLE RIGHT The girth is attached to the straps under the saddle flap on the off side, and then brought under the pony's belly. It is important to ensure that the girth buckles do not bang against the pony's legs.

FAR RIGHT Fastening the girth on the near side. Many ponies blow out their bellies in mild protest at being girthed up, so it is best to fasten the girth only loosely at first, tightening it just before mounting.

for a part-clipped pony (ponies which have been given a full clip need blankets as well), fastened with a roller or surcingle. Trace-clipped ponies at grass are dressed in a waterproof canvas, wool-lined covering called a New Zealand rug, which has a special arrangement of straps round the legs to prevent it from being dislodged in windy weather or when the pony rolls. Recently, variants of the New Zealand rug have become popular; they look rather like equine anoraks.

Clipping takes place only with the first growth of the winter coat (in Britain from September to January or February), after which it is allowed to grow out again. Trimming — removing excess hair from mane and tail, and sometimes from the lower legs and the head — may be done at any time of the year. Again, a pony at grass needs all the protection it can get, so only minimal pulling of the mane is done, and the tail is usually left unpulled, although it may be cut off about 10 cm (4 in) below the hock to prevent it trailing in the mud. Pulling a mane in order to thin it requires skill and patience to avoid causing the pony pain and creating an untidy result. Thinning involves pulling out a few hairs at a time from the underside of the mane, which should never be cut with scissors. The tail, too, may be trimmed to shape at the top by judicious pulling; this *can* result in a tail which resembles an overgrown toothbrush, so expertise is necessary here, too. Tail bandages are used with pulled tails to encourage the short hairs to lie flat and to improve the shape of the tail; while they are less effective on an unpulled tail, they can

help to make it look tidy. Unpulled tails are sometimes plaited, which looks splendid when well done but is far from easy to do. Sometimes a small portion of the mane is removed altogether at the poll to allow the bridle to sit neatly over the top of the head; full removal of the mane, known as hogging, is seldom now carried out except on cobs. Blunt-ended scissors may with care be used to tidy the jaw of a very hairy pony, but the sensitive whiskers round its muzzle are never removed. In summer the lower legs may be trimmed with care if they are very hairy (known as 'carrying a lot of feather'), but in winter the hair protects the legs from mud and is best left alone.

Hoof and Shoe
The horny hoof which forms the 'wall' of the pony's foot grows continuously and needs regularly to be rasped, for much the same reasons as humans file their nails. A pony which is shod needs to have its shoes removed, its feet trimmed, and the shoes replaced or renewed by a farrier (the correct name for a blacksmith who specializes in work with ponies and horses) once every month or six weeks; worn or loose shoes require immediate attention. So also do 'risen' clenches, which may cause injury if not dealt with. Clenches are the filed-off ends of the nails holding a shoe onto a pony's foot; a risen clench is one which has come through the surface of the hoof from below. Ponies kept together in a field — and they are much happier in company than alone — often have their hind shoes removed to avoid injury from kicking; a pony which will not be required for work for a long period may have

all its shoes removed. But the unshod feet still require the pony's equivalent of a manicure every six weeks to prevent their splitting or becoming damaged in other ways.

Illness

Ponies are basically extremely healthy animals, rarely suffering from the coughs and colds prevalent among horses, and seldom going lame or contracting diseases. Their well-being of course partly depends on sensible and knowledgeable care; laminitis, already mentioned, is just one example of a disease which may be caused by misplaced kindness. There is, of course, always the possibility of a pony wounding itself by treading on a nail, being scratched by a bramble, bruising its foot on a stone, and so on. In addition, there is a small number of other ailments to which a pony may succumb. The most common of these is colic, the pony's version of stomach ache. There are varying degrees of severity in colic, but it is necessary for a vet to examine a pony which has even a mild attack. The symptoms are obvious: the pony will be restless, will look round at its flanks, may try to get down and roll, and may break out into a sweat. Before the vet arrives the best thing to do is to walk the pony quietly and firmly around the paddock or stable yard; if it is allowed to lie down and roll, complications may be caused. The vet generally administers medicine known as a colic drench. There are many causes for colic, notably too much food eaten too quickly, watering after feeding rather than before, and mouldy or otherwise contaminated food.

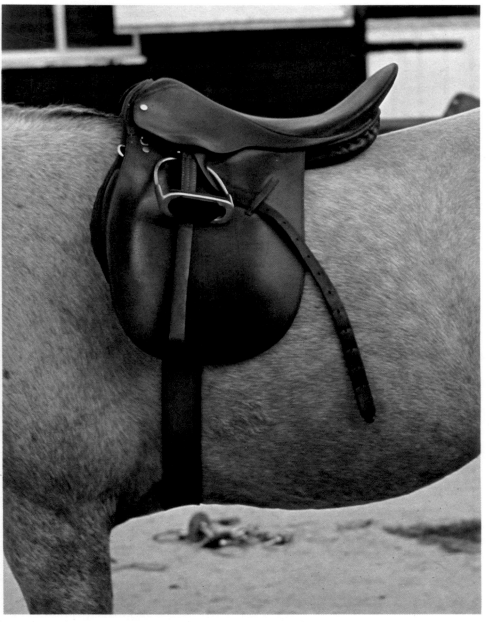

ABOVE The correctly fitted general-purpose saddle.

Almost all ponies suffer from worms, and it is general practice for vets to administer worming powders at regular intervals. Poorly cared-for and over-grazed pasture will give rise to worse attacks of worms, particularly of redworm, the commonest form. The other disease against which all ponies need to be protected is tetanus, or lockjaw, for which injections are available. It can be a by-product of even minor wounds, and regular injections of serum will prevent it occurring. Ponies may also suffer from skin complaints such as lice, ringworm, and sweet itch, all of which can be treated with powders or other medicines. If a pony goes off its food but otherwise seems well, it may need to have its teeth attended to — but this, too, is one of the matters the vet customarily attends to in the course of his regular examination of a pony.

Many ponies go through their entire life without ever becoming ill, and with only occasional accidental lameness. The signs of good or ill health are, with practice, easy to read. A healthy pony will be alert and interested in his surroundings, will have bright eyes, and will stand squarely on all four legs. Sometimes a pony will rest a hind

Putting on the bridle

NEAR RIGHT Care must be taken not to cause the pony any discomfort, or it may become 'head-shy' and difficult to bridle. The bit is placed under the pony's muzzle; an obliging pony will open its mouth willingly to take the bit, but as encouragement to the reluctant a thumb may be inserted between the lips at the mouth bars.

FAR RIGHT The bit is gently lifted into the pony's mouth, without banging the teeth or pinching the lips, and then the headpiece is taken up over the pony's ears.

BELOW RIGHT To make the bridle comfortable, the forelock and mane at the poll should be brought out from under the bridle browband and headpiece. The throatlatch (and noseband, if used) are then fastened.

leg, which is normal, but if it rests a foreleg (by pointing it forward), pain or discomfort is indicated. The pony should be ready for its food, and will eat readily. Its droppings should be well formed, with no mucus or parasites. Its temperature and pulse will be normal, the breathing easy and regular. A healthy pony should have a shining coat, the hairs lying flat and the skin moving easily over the tissues. A dull, staring coat is a sure sign of ill health.

Tack

A visit to a saddler's shop or to a stall at a large show will reveal a bewildering array of saddlery and other equipment for use with horses and ponies. Much of the equipment is specialized and is used only in particular circumstances and in expert hands. The items of tack (as this equipment is usually called) most often found and most generally useful are more limited in range than a saddler's shop might suggest.

The saddle is one of the most important — and most expensive — items of equipment. A good-quality saddle will last for many years; a poor one will need more frequent repair, will wear out more quickly, and, more important, is less likely to be comfortable for either pony or rider. There are many kinds of saddle designed for specific purposes (a racing saddle, for example, is quite different in shape from a dressage saddle), but the commonest type is known as an all-purpose saddle, and much thought has gone into its design in order to make it suitable for most everyday riding activities. Apart from being of good quality, a saddle should fit the pony which has to wear   e saddle must not press on the pony's spine even when the rider has mounted. A groove called the gullet runs along the length of the underside of the saddle to accommodate the spine, but it will do so only if the saddle fits correctly. Secondly, it must clear the withers. The pommel is designed to allow space for the withers, but it must be high enough for a hand to be inserted when the pony's head is in its normal position. A well-made saddle which fits both mount and rider will ensure

a comfortable pony and help the rider to develop a good 'seat' (as the riding position is called); a badly made saddle makes both mount and rider uncomfortable, and is much more difficult to ride well in. The best type are 'spring-tree' saddles, so called because of the springs in the saddle frame, or 'tree'.

Saddles are lined in serge, linen, or leather. Of these, serge is the least satisfactory as it does not wear very well and is difficult to keep clean; linen wears better, is easy to wash, and dries quickly; leather lasts the longest and is the easiest to clean, but it requires more careful attention than the others or it may become hard and make a pony's back sore. The girths, which are passed under the pony's belly and buckle onto the saddle on both sides under the flaps, are made of webbing, nylon or string, or leather. For safety's sake, webbing girths are often used in pairs; nylon girths, which have largely replaced the string girth, are easy to clean, hard wearing, and, as they

RIGHT ABOVE Ponies are happier in company than alone, and may be lonely if kept in a paddock by themselves. When ponies are introduced to each other there may be a slight scuffle at first, but they soon settle down and establish their own hierarchy. Even a pony which appears to be bullied will prefer this state of affairs to isolation.

RIGHT BELOW Much time and energy can be saved if ponies are trained to come when they are called. Guile and patience are needed to catch a reluctant untrained pony. A good method, as here, is to approach it with some nuts in a bowl, rattling them temptingly while keeping the headcollar out of sight.

martingale. There are two principal types: the standard martingale and the running martingale. Both have a looped piece of leather which is attached to the girth between the pony's forelegs and is held in place on the chest by a loop in a strap running round the neck. The standard martingale attaches at its other end to the noseband (a cavesson, never a drop noseband), and if the pony attempts to raise its head too high it will be restrained by the martingale exerting pressure through the noseband. The running martingale divides above the neckstrap into two narrower pieces, each with a ring at the end through which the rein is passed. Its effect is to hold the pony's head down through pressure on the mouth and the poll.

The correct fitting of bits, bridles, and martingales is as important as the fitting of saddles. The bit should be the right width for the pony's mouth: a bit which is either too wide or too narrow will be uncomfortable. Inside the pony's mouth there is a part of the jaw without teeth, known as the 'bars'; it is here that the bit rests. The bridle should be adjusted so that the bit sits in the pony's mouth just wrinkling the corners of the lips: if it is too low it will bruise the pony's mouth; if it is too high it will pinch the corners of the lips. A browband which is too small will pull the headpiece too close to the ears, causing discomfort; a noseband that is too small will rub the pony. Martingales should be fitted so that they exert pressure only if the head is raised excessively high: normal raising and stretching of the head and neck should not be affected.

Looking After Tack

All saddlery will last longer and be safer and more comfortable to use if it is properly cared for. The leatherwork is cleaned by washing it with a damp sponge and then soaping it with saddle soap to keep it supple. Linen saddle linings and string, nylon, or webbing girths should be cleaned with a stiff brush. String and nylon girths may be washed periodically. Metalwork should be cleaned and polished, but the bit mouthpiece should never be shined with any kind of metal polish — the taste invariably distresses the pony. Whenever saddlery is cleaned it should be checked for signs of wear, particularly the stitching on girth straps and stirrup leathers and on bridle leather if the bridle is stitched rather than being of the buckle type. Saddle panels need to be re-stuffed from time to time. Proper handling of saddlery will also help to keep it in good order. The saddle should preferably be kept on a saddle horse; if it is stored on a flat surface it should be stood on end, resting on its pommel.

A last, but vital, piece of standard equipment is the *headcollar*. It should be made of stout leather, must fit the pony snugly, and should be saddle-soaped regu-

larly. Headcollars are used for leading ponies to and from fields, for tying them up in the stable, and at other times when control is required but the pony is not to be ridden. Ponies should always be tied up using a quick-release knot. Many ponies are awkward about being caught in a field, and it is often advisable to leave a headcollar on a pony at grass. The lead rope may have an 'eye' at one end through which the other end of the rope is threaded, or it may have a metal clip. Hemp halters, also often used, have a rope as an integral part; they are less hard wearing than headcollars and cannot be left on a pony in a field.

Saddlery, especially that of good quality, is expensive, but if it is taken care of it will last for many years. Second-hand equipment, however, is often available from saddlers or from owners who may be selling their ponies, and many young riders acquire their first basic items of tack through classified advertisements in the horse and pony magazines. For beginners, indeed, it is an advantage to buy second-hand tack, as new saddles take some time to become soft and comfortable to use.

Riding for Pleasure

Riding used to be considered very much the province of the countryman. The children of farmers might learn how to ride, but once horses and ponies had been replaced by cars and buses for urban transport, most city dwellers lost the habit of riding. During the last 30 years or so the increasing popularity of everything to do with riding and with horses and ponies — due in no small part to the showing of equestrian sports on television — has changed this. It is now easy to find riding schools, in towns as well as in the country, which will give adequate tuition to the complete novice and more advanced lessons to those who need them. It has also, however, become an expensive business to learn how to ride, particularly in towns where rents are high and space is at a premium; it is all the more important, therefore, to ensure that money paid to a riding school is being well spent.

Most riding schools are nowadays run properly, with due care being given to the well-being of the ponies and the enjoyment and instruction of the riders. Some years ago there was an outcry about the conditions prevailing in a minority of riding schools, as a result of which the Riding Establishments Act Committee of the British Horse Society now operates a scheme jointly with local authorities for the inspection and approval of riding schools. The British Horse Society is *the* British riding organization; those interested in riding are sure to benefit from membership. Its headquarters are at the National Equestrian Centre (in Kenilworth, Warwickshire). Among its many activities and services, it will provide a list of approved riding schools. It is wise to attend a riding school at which the instructors have qualified as British Horse Society Assistant Instructors (BHSAI) or Instructors (BHSI); this will ensure that the right methods of riding are taught, and that the instructors, who undergo proper training not only in horsemastership but also in teaching, are professionals. It is also worth finding out whether a particular riding school merely provides quiet ponies for inexperienced riders to sit on, or whether it offers proper lessons in riding as well as in the care of ponies. If the staff is properly qualified, the latter will usually be the case. Local authorities may also be able to provide guidance about the facilities for riding, as for any other sport, in their area.

An assessment of a local riding school may prove difficult for the complete novice to make for himself. But it is possible for even the inexperienced, with a little common sense and some background information, to judge whether a school is being properly run. The ponies should look well fed and cared for, the stables should be clean and in good condition — though they need not necessarily be smart — and the saddlery should be clean and comfortable for the ponies to wear, not hard and stiff and dirty. The ponies should have a reasonable amount of space, not be cramped together; it is better if they are worked on what one might term a shift system, rather than coming in from one ride to be claimed immediately by another rider and taken out again. If the staff are pleasant — both to ponies and to other staff, as well as to clients — and do not seem rushed off their feet, it is a good indication that the ponies are given more careful attention than those in stables which are badly understaffed and where there is inadequate supervision. Some schools cater only for those who want to ride, not for those who would like also to learn a little about the care of ponies; in other words, they teach horsemanship rather than horsemastership. Such schools will be less attractive for people who prefer to know themselves how to remove a pony's tack at the end of a ride, rather than having the pony whisked away by a hurried and officious groom to stables which are out of bounds to riders. For anybody considering having riding lessons as a preliminary to owning a pony, it is of course essential to have proper teaching and experience in the care of ponies. Riding schools which declare that they instruct riders rather than just taking them out for a ride need to have proper facilities for doing so: certainly a field where training sessions can take place, and preferably, in the bigger schools, a covered arena so that lessons can take place in bad weather. It may, however, be as unwise to choose a very grand and advanced riding

ABOVE It is almost never too late to start learning to ride: here a group of beginners of very different ages receives instruction at a riding school in Germany.

RIGHT ABOVE First steps in riding: learning how to mount. This pony is being controlled by a trainer from the lunge, so the rider does not have to worry about the pony as she receives instruction in how to ride.

school for elementary teaching as it is to choose one that does not teach at all; the biggest schools may be so busy coaching their advanced pupils that they ignore beginners.

Riding Clothes

Whatever the occasion — formal or informal, a gentle walk round a paddock or a sustained ride in the country — the right clothing is important and should be chosen with some care. The beautifully cut, made-to-measure, and very smart clothing worn by competitors at the big shows need not even be considered by the novice rider. There are, however, sound reasons underlying most of the clothing that riders wear, and some items are essential. The most important parts of the body, as far as riding gear is concerned, are the head and the feet. For anybody intending to ride at all seriously, a hard riding hat is a must. It should be what is known as a hunting or jockey cap — a velvet-covered peaked cap, hard in structure to protect the head in case of a fall. The cap should fit well enough not to fall off of its own accord, even when the head is held upside down, and should be black or navy blue in colour. Caps in more garish colours, although they may be structurally sound, are generally frowned upon.

Footwear is also important for safety reasons: a soft shoe without a heel prevents a rider from holding the foot correctly in the stirrup, and the whole foot may slip through the stirrup, which is likely to lead to serious injury. At the least, a pair of stout leather lace-up shoes with a clearly defined heel should be worn. Gumboots are not safe to wear, as they are usually so wide that they are liable to get stuck in the stirrup; there is now available an excellent compromise between gumboots and hunting boots: rubber riding boots, properly shaped like a hunting boot, which are suitable both for riding and doing stable work, and also for catching up ponies from muddy fields. Proper hunting boots, also inappropriate wear for the novice, are made of leather reaching to the knee, and are worn with breeches. Apart from the rubber riding boots, jodhpur boots remain the most popular footwear. These are ankle boots designed to be worn with jodhpurs (see below), and have either an elasticated strip in the side or a strap which buckles round the ankle. They are light and comfortable to wear, but do not keep out the wet very well — they were originally designed for use in India during the dry seasons.

Sitting in a saddle for any length of time can be very uncomfortable if suitable trousers are not worn. Best of all are proper jodhpurs, a sort of trouser, which are narrow from the knee down, fitting snugly to the calf and ankle. When properly fitted,

they will not wrinkle or ride up the leg, and are extremely comfortable to wear. They used to be made of thick twill and were therefore hot in warm weather and difficult to clean; they are now available in cotton and man-made stretch mixtures which can be washed in a machine and are light to wear while retaining the good qualities of the old-fashioned variety. Jodhpurs are fawn or creamy-coloured. If it is not possible to buy a pair of jodhpurs, then ordinary trousers may be worn, but they should be fairly thick (tough denim will do), and should preferably fit closely, but comfortably, around the leg. Only one experience with the wrong sort of trousers will be needed before a more suitable alternative is sought: the inside of the rider's legs and the posterior will probably be rubbed raw, and having skin pinched by stirrup leathers is also very painful. Even thick denim jeans are useless if they have the usual broad, raised seam on the inside of the legs for these, too, will rub painfully.

For formal riding, a tweed hacking jacket is a neat, warm top covering over a shirt and tie. For ordinary riding a polo-neck sweater or cotton shirt, and an anorak for windy or wet weather, are perfectly suitable. It is best to avoid lurid colours when choosing ordinary clothes to wear for riding: turquoise and purple, jungle prints, and seaside stripes look curiously out of place, while the

country colours — quiet greens, beige, brown, grey, and so on — and dark colours such as blue and black are all more acceptable. For some reason yellow and red, though both are bright, are also generally regarded as acceptable. For those who ride regardless of the weather, and live in wet areas, a worthwhile investment will be a

ABOVE Leading a pony in hand. The leader moves in line with the pony's shoulder, using the lead rope or, as here, the leading rein merely to guide and control the pony, not to drag it forward.

ABOVE Working on the lunge. This is good training both for the pony, which learns to move correctly on the circle and thus build up its muscles, and for the rider, who is able to perform suppling and balancing exercizes to improve her seat while the pony is under the trainer's control.

RIGHT ABOVE Trotting over poles laid on the ground is the first lesson in jumping for both pony and rider. It teaches the pony to pick up its feet and to trot in rhythm. Poles and cavalletti used in this way also help to prevent the pony from rushing at its fences.

RIGHT BELOW This pony, which has obviously been carefully trained, is jumping freely and cleanly over quite a sizeable fence. The rider, although she should be looking ahead towards the next fence rather than at the ground, is jumping well 'with' (in balance with) her pony.

proper riding mackintosh. This is particularly hard-wearing and waterproof, and like a New Zealand rug has a special arrangement of straps which buckle round the legs, thus keeping the rider's thighs — and the saddle — dry, even in the most persistent rain.

Some people happily ride without gloves except in the coldest weather; others wear them whenever they ride, however hot it may be. Gloves help to prevent the reins slipping when they are wet — either from rain or from sweat on a pony's neck — and also protect the rider's hands. It is best, again, to buy proper riding gloves, which are made of 'string', sometimes lined with wool for warmth; like jodhpurs and riding mackintoshes, they should be fawn-coloured, or cream or yellow.

A riding hat and proper footwear are essential; for everyday riding, the rest of the rider's equipment is largely a matter of choice and the size of his purse, although some of the smarter riding schools may expect conventional clothing to be worn, and for gymkhanas, Pony Club rallies, riding club or other gatherings it will also be needed. In general, the aim is one of neatness: bell-bottomed trousers, flapping cardigans, and flowing hair are out of place,

while a neat pair of trousers and a polo neck sweater need cost nothing extra and will look perfectly suitable.

Pony Trekking
Before embarking on a series of lessons, which will cost a good deal of money, it may be a good idea for a prospective rider to have a holiday with ponies to see whether the desire to ride is likely to be a long-lasting one. One of the best ways for the completely inexperienced to do this is to go pony trekking. *Trek* is a word borrowed from Afrikaans, and means to make a journey, although trekking at its simplest, as a holiday activity, is more of a meander. The popularity of trekking has increased enormously in recent years all over the world, but it is unfortunately all too easy to find poor trekking establishments, where the ponies are overworked and badly cared for or neglected and the riders are not properly supervised. In Britain, the best plan is to benefit from the approval scheme run by an organization called Ponies of Britain, and to ensure that any trekking establishment which is being considered is on their list.

For those who have never ridden at all, the morning after the first ride may come as something of a shock: most people, even

ABOVE The National Equestrian Centre at Kenilworth, Warwickshire, is the headquarters of many of the British riding organizations. This indoor riding school is one of the centre's excellent training facilities for both riders and mounts.

RIGHT The Riding for the Disabled organization offers an opportunity to many children who have never been able to take part in any sport. The ponies are very carefully selected for this work, as they must be totally reliable and steady.

riding quietly at a walk through the countryside, find that they are stiff the next day, and can feel muscles which they never even knew existed. It is as well to get as fit as possible before going on a trekking holiday.

Trekking is a splendid way to see unspoilt countryside and to experience the feeling of freedom that riding, even at a very slow pace, can give. A good trekking establishment will take some care in matching riders and ponies so that even very inexperienced riders will feel confident. They will also take the trouble to teach some of the elementary aspects of handling a pony: how to catch and lead it, how to put on its tack and take it off again after a ride, how to mount and dismount properly rather than allowing riders to scramble aboard, and how to sit correctly in the saddle. More than this they are unlikely to teach, and from the point of view of the trek itself it is probably not necessary to do so. The ponies used for trekking are very quiet, and most trekking is done at a walk, perhaps with the occasional trot for riders who are able to manage this.

Most trekking is arranged on a daily basis: the ride will take about a day, with a break for a picnic, and the route is chosen so that the trek ends back at the stables. Post-trekking, on the other hand, takes place over several days with overnight stops on the way. This slightly more ambitious

way of riding is for the adventurous rider with perhaps a little previous experience. So, too, are holidays at establishments which offer 'riding holidays' proper; this is more like spending a week or so at a riding school, with riding and instruction filling each day.

The best riding schools will all take the trouble with new clients to find out at the beginning how much they know. If complete novices are simply told that it is time to saddle up, or even that their ponies are ready 'tacked up' in their boxes and should be led out and mounted, the most likely response is bewilderment. Much of the early confusion can be reduced if first-time riders are allowed to spend some time at the stables just watching what others are doing and, while not getting too much in the way, being allowed to ask questions and familiarize themselves with the stable's routine. Much can be learnt by an observant bystander about the way ponies are handled. Some schools encourage working pupils: in return for tuition in management and riding, pupils spend some time actually helping with the ponies. This is very good experience, but can be an unsatisfactory arrangement unless the pupil is prepared to work consistently and the staff of the school are in their turn prepared to teach the pupil properly and give him or her a fair reward in riding lessons.

ABOVE The Pony Club gives instruction in horsemastership — the care of ponies — as well as in riding. This roan pony is being bandaged with stable bandages lined with gamgee in a demonstration on stable management.

Ponies, even riding-school ponies used to most eventualities, are easily startled by sharp, sudden movements. Those handling them should always speak to a pony before approaching one, perhaps to saddle it, lead it out of the stable, or to pick up a foot or when beginning to groom. The learner-rider should do the same. Before mounting a pony, it is worth spending a few moments becoming acquainted with it; ponies generally respond to the sound of the human voice, and while they do not understand

words, the tone of a voice indicates to them whether the rider is pleased or angry, reassuring and friendly or perhaps nervous and unsure. A rider who dithers may make a pony nervous: firmness is needed in handling, coupled with steady kindness. It is not a good idea to feed titbits to ponies — particularly sweet foods such as sugar — as they may come to expect them and may turn nasty when they are not provided. A few nuts, or a handful of grass, at the end of a ride is reward enough.

Learning to Ride

The first lessons in riding involve learning how to mount and dismount, how to hold the reins, and the correct position in the saddle. Mounting is always done from the pony's 'near' side, the left-hand side (the right-hand side of a pony being known as the 'off' side). This is also the side from which to lead a pony. Learning to mount and to dismount without upsetting the pony in any way by, for example, landing with a heavy bump in the saddle or administering a kick by

mistake, requires care and some agility at first; but it soon becomes habit. A good seat, as the rider's position in the saddle is called, is harder to acquire and may take years of practice to perfect; even professional riders regularly do exercises to maintain their position in the saddle. The aim is to achieve what is known as an 'independent' seat — that is, one which is independent of the stirrups and, in particular, of the reins. Much time during early riding lessons should be spent riding without stirrups at

ABOVE The general aims and principles on which the Pony Club is based are followed in branches all over the world. Here members of the Cobbity Pony Club, New South Wales, are schooling their ponies in jumping.

65

RIGHT Nowadays there are riding schools within reach of most townspeople. Even in central London there is a number of riding schools offering both hacking facilities and tuition. Here a group of riders crosses Bayswater Road on its way to Hyde Park.

the walk and trot (very uncomfortable at first), and without holding the reins, so that the rider learns not to 'hang onto' the reins when he or she feels in danger of losing balance. Riding instructors also encourage other exercises — touching toes, raising the hands above the head, leaning backwards to lie along the pony's back, and many more — to encourage riders to develop a firm seat.

It is worth taking pains from the outset when learning to ride to do so in the correct way. The riding position is likely to feel very strange at first, but watching a good rider and a bad one will show how important it is to learn to ride the right way: a good rider looks at one with the pony; they move together without any lurching or loss of balance, developing a harmony which a bad rider will never achieve. A good instructor will encourage new riders to hold the reins correctly, to keep their heads up and their backs straight, to look ahead, to adjust their stirrups to the correct length (when the leg is allowed to dangle out of the stirrup, the base of the stirrup iron should be on a level with the ankle bone), and to hold their lower legs at the correct angle. At first there will be a lot to remember even at the walk; and it will be lost again at trot, when the greatest effort has to be made in order to learn how to 'rise' with each stride instead of bumping up and down in the saddle. The canter comes

easily after this; and as the first lessons in jumping are conducted at trot and a slow canter, there is no reason why a keen and interested rider should not quite soon be trotting over poles on the ground.

Both during lessons and in books on how to ride, much time and space are likely to be devoted to the *aids*. The aids are the signals a rider uses to tell the pony what it is to do: to go faster (a change of pace is called a 'transition'), to turn, to halt, and so on. The natural aids are the rider's hands, legs, seat, and voice; artificial aids are whips, spurs, and martingales. A fully trained dressage horse with an expert rider will perform the various movements and changes of pace

without any apparent signals being given by the rider; in fact signals *are* being given, but with such finesse and refinement that they are invisible to an observer. Such subtlety is rare, but it can be fascinating to watch and shows what can be achieved. Some riding-school ponies, it must be admitted, are so bored and sluggish that the only way to keep them moving seems to be a constant barrage of kicking; unfortunately, in the long term the more kicking they receive the less notice they take of it; and it is also difficult for a rider to maintain a good seat if constant kicking is necessary. On a well-trained and reasonably energetic pony, a firm squeeze of the legs will achieve what violent kicking

67

rider to present a harmonious whole, a pair working together. The rider should move with the pony's movements rather than bumping about in the saddle regardless of what the pony is doing, and should be aware of the adjustments in balance that the pony has to make in different circumstances. This is done by the rider keeping his weight over the pony's centre of balance, which shifts depending on the pace (walk, trot, or canter) at which the pony is moving and the sort of terrain. Much of the schooling work — that is, formal training of rider and pony — will help to make riding out, either in the country proper or in town parks, on commons, and so on (known as hacking), more pleasant for both. A pony which is obedient to the aids, and a rider who knows how to apply them, will be able to open and close gates without any trouble; a rider who understands a little about the way a pony moves and balances itself will be a more sensitive rider, and the pony will not tire so quickly. When riding uphill, for example, the rider should lean forward slightly, as the pony's hindquarters have enough work to do propelling the pony uphill without having to contend with the rider's weight as well; when riding downhill, the rider should lean very slightly backwards to free the pony's forehand. Over rough terrain it is better to loosen the reins a little and allow the pony to pick its own way over boulders, potholes, or other obstacles, rather than trying to guide it: the pony will be better than its rider at finding the safest path.

When riding outside the confines of a school or on land owned by the school, riders should be courteous to others and also obey both the Highway Code and the unwritten laws of the countryside. When riding on roads, a group of riders should keep together and ride in single file on the same side of the road as other traffic travelling in the same direction (in Great Britain on the left, in most other countries on the right). Hand signals should be given when turning and to wave on other cars; if drivers slow down when passing ponies, they should always be thanked. In the country, riders should not behave as though they had a right to ride over the land; it is best to stick to bridle paths, but where riding across farmland is unavoidable riders should keep to the edges of fields (known, particularly with ploughed fields, as 'riding round the headland'), make quite sure that they do not disturb any livestock, and shut all gates that they find shut. Frequently one reads instructions to people in the country to shut *all* gates; but a farmer who has left a gate open to allow his stock to graze in two adjoining fields will not appreciate having an open gate closed for him. When in doubt, it is better to close a gate than to leave it open, and certainly all gates which are found shut should be firmly fastened again after the riders have passed through.

ABOVE Competitors (both ponies and riders) in every type of gymkhana event need to practise if they are to have much chance of getting among the prizes. Such events often require riders to perform antics that would be quite unfamiliar, and therefore frightening, to an inexperienced pony. That is obviously not the case in this practice session: the well-trained pony seems quite unconcerned by the sight of its rider hopping about in a sack.

RIGHT Most branches of the Pony Club either have access to permanent cross-country courses or have built their own. The Pony Club one-day events and hunter trials enable young riders, such as this girl jumping into a wood, to gain invaluable experience in junior events. Many of the best-known international three-day event riders began their careers in this way.

achieves on a desensitized animal; disobedience — ignoring the aid given as well as actively attempting to do something else — is better countered with a single sharp tap with a stick and a spoken reprimand, than by repeated squeezing and then kicking and more kicking.

The hands should also be used quietly and gently. Unless it has been deadened by years of careless handling, a pony's mouth is extremely sensitive. Those who train young ponies know that only the slightest pressure is required, although the pony may not understand what it is being asked to do. A pony which pulls is often reacting to feelings of pain or discomfort in its mouth; tugging at the reins, or putting a more severe bit on a pony which pulls, is more likely to aggravate the problem than to alleviate it, as the more pain that it feels the harder will the pony try to get away. Rather than expecting a pony to realize that it is caught in a vicious circle, it is up to the rider to use his intelligence, perhaps even by putting a milder bit in the pony's mouth.

The aim in riding is for the pony and its

ABOVE The Pony Club's work is by no means limited to instruction in riding and pony care: this musical ride, typical of the club's more informal activities, involves a display in fancy dress. Note that the riders have taken the wise precaution of wearing riding hats underneath their Red Indian feathered headdresses.

The Pony Club

For those who have had a successful course of riding lessons and who would like to learn more about both horsemanship and horse-mastership (as they are always known, even though it may be ponies being ridden and cared for), and who are under 21 years of age, the best organization to join is the Pony Club. For those over 21 there is an adult equivalent, though a less cohesive organization than the Pony Club, of individual riding clubs affiliated to the British Horse Society; together they are known as 'the Riding Clubs'. The Pony Club was founded in 1929, and apart from the war years 1939-45 has flourished, growing all the time into the international organization it has now become. Many top international riders have been members of the Pony Club, and many attribute their success in part to having belonged to this excellent organization. The first branches of the Pony Club were all attached to hunts, as it was felt that these would cover the most appropriate areas of the country. With the remarkable growth of interest in riding since World War II this has changed, and branches are now to be found everywhere in Britain — and in Australia, Canada, Singapore, and Holland, to name but a few of the other countries which have set up Pony Clubs of their own.

The Pony Club also caters nowadays for those who do not own their ponies — another change to take account of the increasing number of children interested in riding but who do not have the facilities, expertise among the family, or the money to buy and keep a pony of their own.

The activities of the Pony Club are numerous. The aim is to teach young riders how to care for their ponies, and how to ride them well in order to get the best out of them. There are branch events all through the school holidays, and in some areas also at weekends in term times. These events begin with instructional rallies, at which the theory and practice of schooling a pony and riding it, and jumping and preparing for gymkhanas and other competitions are taught. Members are divided into 'rides', so that everybody is grouped with others who have equal experience and ability. Teaching is also given on how to groom ponies and fit and clean tack, how to deal with the common ailments, understanding the principles of feeding, and so on. Proficiency tests are held, from the elementary 'D' test up to the advanced 'A' test (generally taken only by associate members, those between 17 and 21 years of age), in which a thorough knowledge and understanding of horsemas-tership is required. The syllabus of Pony

Club teaching and the knowledge demanded by these tests are contained in the *Manual of Horsemanship,* which is the official handbook of the Pony Club and of the British Horse Society. The Pony Club is run under the aegis of the BHS, and details about it can be obtained from the National Equestrian Centre at Kenilworth.

In addition to rallies, the Pony Club organizes numerous other events. Every summer a week-long camp, often residential, is held, where instruction is combined with such relaxing occupations as film shows, quiz competitions, mounted wild-goose chases, and an open day at the end of the week. Lectures, visits to the local hunt kennels, and other outings are also arranged. Last, but by no means least, the

Pony Club is responsible for all sorts of competitive events, including the Mounted Games Championship, with the coveted Prince Philip Cup being awarded to the victorious team after finals held each year at the Horse of the Year Show. The local hunter trials and one-day events (a scaled-down version of the adult three-day events for combined training — dressage, cross-country, and show jumping) culminate in the inter-branch championship, a stiff one-day event at which only the best riders and most highly-trained ponies can hope to do well. With proper Pony Club tuition and plenty of practice, however, every rider can achieve what the Pony Club sets out to attain: a reasonable level of all-round, thoughtful horsemanship.

ABOVE The annual Pony Club Camp often ends with a prize-giving ceremony. Not only those with the best ponies and most experience win prizes: there are awards for clean tack and for improvement at all levels, as well as for the winners of competitions. This photograph gives a good idea of the friendly informality of Pony Club gatherings.

71

Shows and Showing

One of the best-filled in-hand classes at the Dublin Horse Show is that for Connemaras, Ireland's own native pony breed. The show is regarded as the country's foremost shop window for horses and ponies, and the pony which wins this class is almost assured of a successful career.

PAGES 74-5 A scene of organized chaos typical of many shows. In the foreground, a form of bending race, involving caps hung on the poles, is in progress; in another arena in the background, a show-jumping course has been erected.

The first-time visitor to a horse show may be confused by the variety of events taking place, and feel as though he has walked into an Alice-in-Wonderland scene in which everybody except him knows what is going on and how to appreciate it. Shows can be very enjoyable occasions; but, as with all competitive sports, the enjoyment is greatly increased if one has some idea of what is happening.

Most shows are organized along similar lines, whether the occasion is a small local gymkhana catering for young children or a large county show combining equestrian events with competitions for cattle, sheep, dogs, and flower arrangers. Most shows have an organizing committee whose members are responsible for planning the show and ensuring that it runs smoothly, and a show secretary to co-ordinate the work. Even at a small show arrangements need to be made to mark out the arenas, to provide seating for spectators, to handle car parking and admittance payments, and to provide refreshments. In addition, the show must be advertised in good time so that potential competitors will decide to attend in large enough quantities to make the show a success. Programmes must be drawn up and printed, giving a variety of events to please both competitors and spectators, and allowing enough time for each class to be judged. Entry forms need to be sorted, the entrance fees checked and dealt with, judges appointed, prizes provided, and stewards, car park attendants, and other officials properly informed about the lines on which the show is to be run.

There are various organizations in Britain connected with the show world. The native-pony-breed societies are involved with breed classes whose principal aim is to maintain the quality of each particular breed; in addition to these there are the Arab and the hack and cob breed societies, the Hunters Improvement and Light Horse Breeding Society (generally known as the HIS), the National Pony Society and the Ponies of Britain, and the British Show Pony Society. Many shows are affiliated to the various organizations, not only for show classes but also for jumping (controlled by

the British Show Jumping Association) — a topic discussed in the next chapter.

For a show to be a success, regardless of its size and scope, it must make money, or at the least cover its costs. Money is raised by donations and sponsorships, by charging entrance fees for competitors, exhibitors, spectators, and their cars, by advertising in show programmes, by the lease of concessions to catering companies to provide refreshments and to other shops, and by societies and organizations which may set up stalls on the showground. One of the important functions of show organization is to ensure a programme which will both provide a challenge and wide range of classes to tempt competitors to enter, and supply a varied and entertaining day out for the spectators, only a small proportion of whom will consist of the admiring friends and families of those competing or of others who are knowledgeable about the finer points of horsemanship. Like the village fete, the local gymkhana is a high spot in the calendar for any area, much looked forward to by all concerned. The larger shows will attract competitors and spectators from a wider area, shows at county level and upwards drawing people from all over the country and also from abroad. To compete in the top shows such as the Royal International Horse Show it is necessary to qualify by winning specific events at other shows during the season.

Showing Classes

The most serious element in the various events held at shows is contained in the showing classes, so it is perhaps appropriate to consider these in some detail. The aim of these classes is to improve the quality of a particular breed or type of horse or pony and to provide a shop window, and to some extent a market place, for breeders and trainers. Most shows have classes for both ponies and horses, and while these differ in points of detail much the same basic rules and principles apply.

Pony show classes are of various kinds. They begin with leading-rein classes for small children who are able to ride with the help of an adult but are not yet old or capable

ABOVE A group of well-behaved youngstock being shown in hand. Show-ring experience of the right sort will stand a youngster in good stead, but he will need to be properly handled before being entered for a show: even among yearlings, bad behaviour in the ring is heavily penalized by the judges.

enough to be able to handle a pony entirely on their own. These ponies need to be quiet and well behaved rather than beautiful, although a good-looking pony in this class will always win over an equally docile but less handsome animal. In all the pony classes the judges must take into account the importance of behaviour and of a pony's suitability to be ridden by a child; although where competition is fiercest, among the larger ponies and older children, this point may sometimes be overlooked. Other general classes are to be found with such titles as 'novice pony', 'first riding pony', and so on, with various stipulations in the rules governing eligibility.

The most important classes for children's riding ponies are those governed by the ponies' height and, secondarily, the age of the riders. The height divisions for these classes are: up to 12.2 hands; 12.2 hands but not exceeding 13.2 hands; and over 13.2 but not exceeding 14.2 hands. It is in these classes that the most beautiful show ponies are to be found. The standard of children's riding ponies has risen very noticeably since the sport of showing began to gain popularity in the years after World War II, and at the larger shows one commonly sees some children's ponies of outstanding quality. There seems also to be a changing fashion among show ponies. Some years ago it was considered that substance was required, as the majority of ponies were expected to be suitable for hunting; now a lighter, more refined pony is generally the more popular type, with the substance being found in working-pony classes rather than in the true show classes. Since the breeding of show ponies became almost an industry, and to win in the show ring the aim of families with a good deal of money, it has become commonplace for top-class show ponies to change hands for enormous sums. By the same token, however, the extreme beauty and high cash value of these ponies

has begun to make some of them unsuitable as children's ponies: they are too costly an investment to be subjected to the rough and tumble of everyday riding, Pony Club rallies, riding picnics, paperchases, and the many other entertaining forms of riding preferred by most children, and their use tends to be limited to performances in the ring. Moreover, once winning prizes becomes the only aim for the owner, ponies may be bred to a point of such refinement that they become like miniature Thoroughbreds, and lose the pony temperament which has contributed so much to children's enjoyment. At some shows older children or lightly built adults can be seen 'riding in' such ponies, and only when the edge has been taken off their energy will the young entrants be put in the saddle.

The vast majority of ponies at almost all shows are still, however, good all-round ponies, though they have more quality than

assistant, who comes into the ring at that moment armed with a brush and stable rubber to smooth away saddle marks from the pony's coat), and each pony in turn is led out in hand, stands in front of the judges for another assessment of the pony's conformation, and is then made to walk away from the judges and trotted back towards and past them. This gives the judges the opportunity to scrutinise the pony's movement from both in front and behind to see whether it moves straight. It is another important test of the quality of preparation that has been put in at home, for a pony which has been taught to lead in hand properly is more likely to move straight and true than one which is being dragged along behind its rider. The pony should move on a loose rein, its rider running along level with its shoulder. Finally, the ponies are re-saddled and remounted, and the judges will ask the riders to walk them round the ring again before they make their final decision on the

winner and those who are to be placed second, third, and so on.

Other Show Classes

These procedures are followed, with variations, for all ridden show classes. Most shows hold classes for hacks and perhaps for cobs, and also for hunters. In the hunter classes the judges ride the horses as well as looking at them. A skilful and experienced show rider may be able to conceal minor faults in his horse's performance and general behaviour, but they are almost certain to be detected by the judges when they get into the saddle. Hunter classes are also divided, this time into 'lightweight', 'middleweight', and 'heavyweight' classes; an additional class sometimes featured by the big shows is one for ladies' hunters, some of which are still ridden side-saddle: a splendid sight, less familiar nowadays than it once was. While the requirements in these classes are rather different from those of the

ABOVE Another handsome show pony. Although few people ride side-saddle nowadays, in the formal surroundings of the show ring it can look very effective. The pony's stitched show bridle, a lighter version of the ordinary double bridle, helps to show off its head to best advantage.

pony classes, the criteria of the judges are much the same: first-class conformation, smoothness at all paces, obedience, and condition. In the hack classes, obedience and elegance are of paramount importance in horses which, as they are bred for leisurely riding, need less substance than that expected of a hunter, but should make up for this by superb quality and presence.

For those with ponies which are not quite fine enough to be successful in the show ring but are nevertheless nicely made and good performers, the working-pony classes have been a welcome innovation. In these classes ponies are asked to jump a course of perhaps six fences, in the show ring but over natural-looking jumps (for example, brush fences and 'rustic' unpainted poles), as well as being judged on conformation and show. Many of the best *children's* ponies, as opposed to the most beautiful ponies, are to be found in these classes — and those competing, while they may appear just slightly less 'professional' than the true show rider, are often better all-round riders and enjoy competing for its own sake as well. Hunters are catered for in the working-hunter class, which is run on the same lines as the working-pony class.

Conformation is also the prime consideration in the other show classes: the breed classes, and those for youngstock. There are show classes for both ridden horses and ponies, and for in-hand stock; unlike the show pony and show hunter classes, breed-class entrants are always shown with 'full' (unplaited) mane and tail. Arabs, palominos, spotted horses, and so on are catered for as well as native British pony breeds; so, too, are the heavy-horse breeds, which are making a welcome comeback. The youngstock classes are divided by age: there are classes for mares and foals, in which both are judged, and for yearlings, two-, and three-year-olds, all of which are shown in hand.

For those wishing to learn how to judge a good pony, the show classes can be fascinating to watch. They are, however, perhaps most interesting for those involved with ponies and horses rather than the pure spectator, for whom some of the other events at shows provide better entertainment. For the serious pony lover, a study of the way a pony looks and moves, and an assessment of why a judge has placed one pony higher than another, will be an excellent lesson in acquiring an 'eye' for a pony. And not always the same pony wins: judges differ in their views and preferences, and like humans, ponies can have an off day, when the sparkle which makes a pony catch the judges' eye may be missing.

Sporting events — show jumping and gymkhana events — which take place at shows will be dealt with in the next chapter. Apart from these events, and the show classes, there are other classes which are a delight to both the competitors and the spectators. One of these is the fancydress class. It is not necessary for competitors in this class to have either a handsome pony or

one that performs brilliantly; as long as the pony is obedient enough not to constitute a danger to other competitors, it will stand as good a chance of winning as any other. An enormous amount of ingenuity goes into making the costumes for both ponies and riders. Again, however, time needs to be spent at home familiarizing a pony with its costume, and ensuring that, however elaborate the costume maye be, it does not interfere with the rider's need to be in full control of his or her mount. These colourful classes provide a good deal of fun for all concerned.

Excitement is also provided by the harness classes. Britain has a long history of coaching, and the days when all travelling took place by coach and horses, there were sporting clubs which organized races from city to city or from house to house, betting large sums of money on the outcome. With the introduction of railways, driving went into a decline, and then almost disappeared after the invention of the internal-combustion engine and the advent of the motor car. Very recently there has been a renewed interest in driving in harness, and this has been reflected in the number of classes held at shows. These range from single and tandem classes for ponies,

ABOVE These beautifully matched road ponies should do well in show-pony pairs classes. In these events not only colour and type but also such factors as length of stride, head carriage, and temperament are taken into account by the judges. An identical turnout for both ponies and riders makes the effect all the more striking.

TOP A competitor in a scurry-driving competition. Small ponies such as these are often the most successful, as their ability to turn tight corners often saves vital seconds on the twisty course.

ABOVE An eye-catching hackney turnout at the Horse of the Year Show. The high head and tail carriage, as well as the high-stepping, exaggerated action, are typical of this dashing and elegant driving pony.

polished down to the last wheel spoke, with matching paint and braid, and drivers appropriately dressed for each class and type of vehicle.

Many shows, particularly the larger ones, also feature parades and displays. These may consist of a musical ride given by the local branch of the Pony Club, a parade of the local hunt, a quadrille dressage display, motorcycle drives, and any other diversions the show organizers are able to think of.

Behind the Scenes

At most shows there are hundreds of competitors, exhibitors, ponies and horses, and grooms and well-wishers, and courtesy between them all is an unwritten law of the showground. The spectators also have a part to play in ensuring that the show runs smoothly. It is the ponies' day, and while riders of course have a duty not to run down spectators, the latter should try to keep out of the way. On the other hand, for those who wish to learn about ponies, much of what is most interesting to watch at shows takes place out of the ring rather than inside it. Each ring — and at the big shows there will be several different arenas in which different events are held simultaneously — has what is known as a 'collecting' ring attached to it, in which competitors await their turn or the next class gathers in order not to waste time during a busy schedule. It is often one of the most rewarding places to watch, as here one sees the competitors off duty, perhaps jumping over practice fences or schooling their ponies before entering the ring, making last-minute adjustments to saddlery, and receiving final instructions on what to do and what not to do. It is not, however, appreciated if spectators enter the collecting ring itself, and most competitors there are likely to appear rather off-hand if they are spoken to. This is not intentional rudeness but an expression of tension on the part of those about to compete, who need to retain their concentration for the job in hand. Patting ponies without asking to be allowed to do so is not encouraged, and they should never be fed titbits by well-meaning onlookers.

A discreet stroll around the horseboxes, when this is permitted by the show authorities, can also be fascinating. Boxes and trailers are usually parked a little way away from the bustle of the showground, and here the real work is going on: ponies being lunged (see next chapter), plaits which have come undone being resewn, brushing and polishing and adjusting — and afterwards, the relaxation that comes with knowing that it is over, ponies being unsaddled, watered and fed, excited congratulations for those who have won and commiserations for those who have not. This is where the real companionship — and the intense, if friendly, rivalries — of the show world are to be found.

through the hackney classes, to marathon drives out on the road (after which the carriages are driven back to the ring for the final judging), and the scurry driving, one of the most popular classes, at which the native ponies seem to excel. To see a pair of ponies swirling round the markers at a neat gallop to complete the course in record time is an exhilarating sight. At the other extreme are the heavy horses, with their beautifully braided manes and tails, which so often parade at shows. Shires, Clydesdales, and Suffolk Punches used to be the pride of Britain's farms, and with their dignified yet generous character and impressive stature they are a marvellous sight. In between these two extremes the 'trade-turnout' classes, with smart, high-stepping ponies and gaily painted commercial delivery wagons and carts, add colour and variety. In all the harness classes the quality of the turnout is an important aspect of the judging, so every entry is highly

ABOVE Trotting and pacing races have long been popular in the United States, Australia, and in some countries of continental Europe. After slow beginnings, the sport is now becoming established in Britain: this pair of pacers, hobbled to encourage them not to break stride, are performing at the Three Counties Show.

LEFT The driving classes are popular at shows in many countries. This pair of Haflingers, complete with horse brasses, fly fringes, and a foal, are competing at a driving show at Frauenfeld in Switzerland.

Sporting Ponies

RIGHT One of the best-loved show-jumping personalities of recent years is the pony Stroller, ridden by Marian Coakes (now Marian Mould). Although only 14.2 hands, Stroller competed against — and beat — many of the top international horses.

Equestrian sporting events have their origins in man's ancient and seemingly unquenchable desire to make war on his neighbour. Since very ancient times, when contending armies have made intelligent use of cavalry victory has been most likely to go to the side with the most brilliant horsemen and the finest and best-trained horses. This naturally led to intense rivalry among cavalry units, with each claiming superiority in mounts and horsemanship over its comrades in other regiments. Obviously, the best way to prove such claims was to compete against one's rivals in warlike games. These served not only to rekindle the martial spirit in times of peace but also to keep both men and horses at the peak of fitness. Nowadays, of course, sporting events have attained a universal and independent status. But traditional martial mounted games persist in many parts of the world — from the Russian steppes and Afghanistan, where the fierce sport called *Buzkashi* may still be seen, to Argentina and its ancient game of *pato*.

Modern equestrian sporting events are, of course, much gentler and more formal than such hell-for-leather activities. Moreover, both pony and rider must submit to much training and other preparation merely in order to compete, let alone to have a chance of winning. A pony visiting a showground of any kind for the first time is likely to find it a bewildering and frightening experience. There will be a confusion of noise and movement, perhaps hundreds of other strange ponies, tent canvas flapping, bands playing, flags waving, loudspeakers booming, spectators clapping and cheering, strange smells, and a thousand other distractions. No pony should be expected to compete successfully in such surroundings unless it has previously been introduced to them. A riding-school pony, or any other pony which is kept among a large group in stables where there is always a good deal going on, is likely to be less disturbed than one which leads a more individual and private life; both, however, may be scared the first time they hear a large potato being dropped from a height into a metal bucket — as often happens at a gymkhana.

It is worth visiting a gymkhana or other event before even considering entering one — first without a pony, just to see what is going on; and then with the pony in order to introduce it to the showground and its atmosphere. Much preparation is, of course, done away from the showground as well: loud taped music turned on and off, objects dropped with a clatter into buckets, flags being waved or mackintoshes flapped; all initially at some distance from the pony, and then gradually brought nearer as it becomes accustomed to these alarming sights and sounds. If several ponies can be subjected to this process at the same time, so much the better: their riders will together be able to simulate many of the unfamiliar sights and sounds to be found at competitions. Taking a pony to a showground for a day, and just letting it look and listen, may seem like a day wasted, but when the time comes to compete, that pony will be better able to concentrate than one for which the atmosphere of a show is completely strange and therefore alarming.

At the Gymkhana

Gymkhana events provide perhaps the best form of competition for riders with ordinary ponies that are not particularly beautiful (and are therefore unsuitable for the show ring) and that do not have the ability or training to compete successfully in show jumping or other jumping events. The term *gymkhana* is an adaptation of a Hindustani word and was introduced into the English language in the 1860s by the British living in India. There are many kinds of gymkhana events, some by now traditional favourites, while new ones are also constantly being introduced. In Britain most of these events really are games, often involving apple bobbing, sack races, musical chairs or poles, and other events not exclusive to the pony world. It is not necessarily so elsewhere: in the United States, for example, where riding traditions have a different history, mounted games have more in common with work on ranches, and competitions include such events as cowhide racing, calf roping, and other contests typical of the rodeo; moreover, they

ABOVE The game of *buzkashi* has warlike origins: it used to be played by victorious warriors using one of their captives as victim. Nowadays the carcass of a sheep or goat is used as a 'football' in the game, here being played in Afghanistan.

are held for adults even more than for children, whereas in Britain the gymkhana has become an exclusive province of the young.

Although successful gymkhana ponies can be of any breed or type, certain characteristics are desirable. The most successful gymkhana ponies are generally relatively small; even at the highest level of competition — the finals of the Pony Club

Mounted Games Championship — one sees modestly sized ponies — perhaps of 13.2 rather than 14.2 hands. The essential ingredients in a gymkhana pony are quick-wittedness, agility, obedience, speed over short distances — and what can only be described as a competitive spirit, for the best gymkhana ponies are those which visibly enjoy competing. A small, neat, energetic pony will always win over a larger, slower

animal. Ponies need to be fit to compete, and well-enough schooled to obey instantly whatever aids they are given. They must also, of course, be familiar with the various events. One sometimes sees bewildered ponies being dragged down a line of bending poles, for example, with no idea of what is being asked of them and no training to prepare them for the particular physical demands made by the event. Such ponies will not only fail to win: they will quickly become spoilt and sour, as an over-excited rider is liable to be less than considerate to a pony which is not responding as quickly and intelligently as he thinks it should, even if it is clearly the rider's, not the pony's, fault.

As well, therefore, as the need to acquaint a pony with the general appearance of showgrounds, specific training is required to help both pony and rider do well in

gymkhana events. While the events themselves take many forms, there are in fact only a few basic manoeuvres involved in these competitions. It is worth training a pony to make a rapid start, from rest to canter, first of all by teaching it to make the transition from an energetic walk to a canter without the usual trotting in between. Similarly, the ability to make a sudden halt is useful, and a pony which has been taught this need not suffer from the sore mouth often caused by being yanked to a halt because it is unaccustomed to what is required. The competent gymkhana rider knows how to mount by vaulting onto the pony while it is moving, rather than wasting time by putting a foot into the stirrup; he will also have trained himself to mount not only from the near side but also from the off side of the pony, which may also save a few precious seconds in certain events. The pony is taught to go round things — barrels, poles, and other objects — at close quarters rather than in a wide arc; to keep moving while its rider picks up an object (such as a flag on a stick, or a potato from the top of a pile); and to lead well in hand, again from both the near and the off sides. This is important because many events involve either the pony being led while the rider hops along in a sack, for example, or, in a team event, one rider negotiating an obstacle course while his or her mounted partner leads the pony along the course ready for it to be remounted at the end. In general, a successful gymkhana pony will have been made so familiar with a wide variety of activities that it will not be perturbed even when a new and extraordinary contest is devised and it is asked to perform in a different way.

The rules of gymkhana events and the way they are run are quite simple. Most events entail a starting and a finishing line, and competitors have to complete the various elements in the correct order before crossing the finishing line. The one to do so first is the winner. Many events are run in 'heats' of four or six competitors, and the winners of each heat then compete against each other in a final heat. Because it is time which determines the winner, time is also used to penalise those who make mistakes: for instance, a rider who drops a potato not into the bucket but beside it must dismount, pick up the potato, remount, and throw it accurately into the bucket before cantering back to collect the next potato in the row; the error will have cost the rider crucial seconds. Agility, a steady hand and head, and a good eye are as important to the rider as speed and obedience are in the pony.

Learning to Jump

The great majority of riders sooner or later want to learn how to jump; and soon after that they may well want to compete in jumping events. They are well catered for in terms of competitions; learning to jump takes time, however, and a thorough training is vital to success. The events range from show jumping and working-pony classes through hunter trials to one-day events; while the types of fences vary, the training for all kinds of jumping is very much the same, and similar regulations also apply to the various competitions.

Many ponies are natural jumpers: as well as having an innate ability to jump, they seem to enjoy doing so. Even these ponies, however, need training to make the best of this ability, and to learn to cope with awkward jumps that are specially designed to test their skill. Some care is required when young children are learning to jump. A novice child and a novice pony cannot be expected to teach each other how to jump well — indeed, it is more likely that both

will become sour and disappointed by the experience.

Much of the training given to ponies in jumping in fact takes place 'on the flat', as general schooling is sometimes called. A pony will be able to jump well with a rider on its back only if its muscles have been properly developed and it has learnt about balance and impulsion in its ordinary training. Impulsion is the urge to move forwards, properly controlled; it comes from the quarters when a pony is properly collected and balanced, and it is a vital ingredient of successful jumping. The first lesson 'over fences' consists simply of trotting over poles laid flat on the ground; this teaches the pony balance and rhythm, and to look where it is going. Jumping over *cavalletti* is the next stage. Cavalletti are

stout poles fixed at each end to a cross-piece which raises them just a few inches off the ground. At first these are laid in line, and the pony trots over them without breaking stride (that is, without having to adjust the rhythm of the trot). Gradually, if the pony proceeds without difficulty through these early stages, it will be introduced first to a row of cavalletti with a slightly larger fence (perhaps two cavalletti placed one on top of the other) at the end, then progress to proper, though still small, fences.

Much practice will be needed to ensure that the pony is introduced to all the different types of fences: uprights (such as gates and walls), spread fences (oxers, triple bars), water jumps, coloured poles, combination fences (doubles and trebles) must all be encountered, with the emphasis always

being placed on keeping the pony calm, in balance, and obedient. At each stage it is very important never to 'over-face' the pony by expecting it to jump a height or type of fence for which it is not yet ready. A pony which is to jump successfully requires the ability to gauge the distance before a fence, in order to meet it with the right stride for take-off, and also to jump fences which are placed at awkward distances from or angles to each other. However 'natural' a jumper a pony may be, these abilities are acquired only after long practice.

For the rider, learning to jump also involves understanding the way a pony jumps, to ensure that the rider always jumps 'with' the pony, remaining in balance with it through all phases of the jump, and taking care not to interfere with the pony's movements when, for example, it needs to stretch its neck out on landing. The rider, too, will first be introduced to jumping by trotting over poles and then over cavalletti, and then gradually progressing to the more advanced fences. Much time is devoted to learning to jump without reins or stirrups to enable the rider to maintain an independent seat over fences as well as on the flat. The most common fault among novice riders is that of getting 'left behind', when the rider fails to keep his weight over the pony's centre of balance, and finds that as the pony

lands over the fence he is jerked backwards. This usually results in the rider jabbing the pony in the mouth as he hangs on to the reins in an effort to regain his balance. A neckstrap should always be worn by ponies jumping with inexperienced riders; the neckstrap (or, as a last resort, the pony's mane) should be held as the pony takes off over the fence. A pony which is caused pain every time it jumps will soon refuse to jump at all.

One of the best ways of training ponies and their riders over fences is on the *lungeing* rein. Lungeing is in fact an important element in all stages of training. It involves the pony circling round a trainer, controlled by a long lunge rein made of webbing, which is attached to a special noseband known as a lungeing cavesson. This has a ring on the front of the padded noseband which swivels, allowing the pony to be lunged on both reins — that is, from both the off and near sides. A pony learning to jump will benefit from doing so at first without the weight of a rider on its back; a rider learning to jump will be better able to concentrate on his seat and on negotiating the fence correctly when he does not have to control the pony. This apart, lungeing is an extremely good exercise for all ponies, as working on a circle builds up the muscles, and encourages good balance and full use of

the hocks to obtain impulsion; it invariably plays an important part in the breaking in of youngstock.

Jumping Events

Junior show-jumping competitions are organized along the same lines as those for adults. Thanks to the popularity of show jumping as a spectator sport and the widespread coverage given by television to the major competitions, many people are familiar with the rules governing the events. A course is devised which must be followed according to the numbering of the fences: taking the wrong course is penalised by elimination. A pony which refuses acquires three faults; three refusals also results in elimination. Each time a fence is knocked down four faults are incurred; these are added together but do not at any stage cause elimination. Except in speed competitions, time is a factor only in a timed jump-off, but most competitions do have a 'time allowed', which prevents competitors completing the course at a walk. When all the competitors have jumped the course, those with clear rounds (or, if there are no clear rounds, those with the fewest number of faults) will jump a second time over a shorter course, generally with higher fences, to decide the winner. Sometimes, of course, no jump-off is necessary: there may,

ABOVE A well-coordinated hand-over of the baton in a relay race. Split-second timing, the result of hours of practice, is required if the baton is to be quickly and safely exchanged during these team events.

LEFT A supple and well-trained pony will canter down the line of bending poles, swinging only slightly as it weaves between them, as this pony is doing, and making a neat, tight turn at the top of the line.

ABOVE This pony and its young rider obviously enjoy jumping together, although the jump would have been a little more comfortable for both if the pony had taken off farther from the fence.

for example, be only one clear round, one competitor with perhaps three faults, and a third with eight faults. Sometimes the first jump-off takes place against the clock; on other occasions it becomes the deciding factor only in a second jump-off, if the first jump-off has produced more than one clear round. Some people feel that timed jump-offs among children are not a good idea as they encourage careless riding: riding a course with speed and precision is difficult.

Jumping competitions are divided in order to ensure that ponies and riders of roughly equal experience jump against each other: there are novice classes for those who have never won a jumping class, for example. The British Show Jumping Association (BSJA), the governing body of show jumping in Britain, to which most shows are affiliated and to which it is often necessary to belong in order to compete, also grades ponies according to the amount of money they have won, restricting eligibility to classes according to these grades.

The task of the course builder in any

jumping competition is a difficult one. He must design a course which presents enough problems to make it interesting to ride and to watch; on the other hand, too awkward a course will result in a large number of refusals and knockdowns, which is both discouraging for competitors and makes a slower and less exciting competition from the spectators' point of view. With junior competitions the course builder also has to remember that he is dealing with children of varying experience, whose ponies may be spoilt if too much is asked of them. The fences should look solid — all ponies jump better over such fences than over flimsy ones — but at the same time they need to be inviting, and the course should contain an interesting variety of jumps.

Jumping in the show ring requires a slightly different technique from jumping cross-country fences. The course at a hunter trial, for instance, will consist of natural-looking fences, the majority of which really are solid: if a timber fence is knocked it is more likely merely to bruise the pony

slightly than to fall over. Ponies should become accustomed to jumping these types of fences before competing; the practice for such jumping best comes from riding in the country and jumping over any small obstacles that can be found: fallen tree trunks, sheep hurdles and feeding troughs, and low posts and rails are all suitable as long as they are free of wire and other potentially dangerous attachments. The pony must be thoroughly schooled in jumping through water as well as over it; many otherwise competent competitors are eliminated at jumps involving water, of which the majority of ponies are inclined to be suspicious. Hunter trials are held over open country, so the course may include jumping into and out of woodland, up and down hills, through farmyards, over ditches — any of the hazards likely to be found when riding in the country may be encountered. Many Pony Club and riding-club branches, and also the larger riding schools, have their own permanent cross-country courses, which provide a perfect substitute for those

who do not have access to real country riding — or permission from farmers to ride over their land.

A show-jumping course covers a small area and involves twists and turns, the jumping being done from a fairly collected canter. A hunter-trial course, held over quite a large area of land, involves galloping across fields from fence to fence. In order to take the least out of itself and yet to make good time, a pony needs to be fit enough to be able to maintain a steady speed (not a headlong gallop) over some distance, to jump 'in its stride' over the straightforward fences, and not to fight its rider when asked to slow down when approaching a tricky one. The latter may be an 'in-and-out' fence, usually a square of sheep hurdles into which competitors must jump, make a turn, and jump out again at right-angles; it may be a narrow stile or a hunting gate; or it may be an ordinary gate that must not be jumped but opened, passed through, and closed.

Jumping hunter-trial courses is good experience for one of the three phases of a

ABOVE The senior Pony Club one-day events are virtually on the scale of adult competitions, and only thoroughly competent and determined competitors are likely to do well in them. This is a very good jump: controlled but free, with rider and mount jumping in harmony over a very sizeable log fence.

ABOVE A young rider emerging from a wood on the cross-country course at a Pony Club event held in Dorset.

CENTRE Athletic ability as well as riding skill is required in gymkhana events. These are members of Pony Club teams competing in the finals of the inter-branch mounted-games championship for the Prince Philip Cup. The finals are held each year at the Horse of the Year Show.

NEAR RIGHT One of the commonest features of riding-club contests is the quadrille dressage display. Although the riders and their mounts are decked out in colourful and amusing costumes the event involves a serious display of dressage movements. This beautifully turned out quartet are members of the East Grinstead Riding Club.

FAR RIGHT The jumping arena at Hickstead, run for many years by Douglas Bunn, holds competitions at all levels for both children and adults. This young rider is competing on the permanent showground.

combined-training event, as one-day events (and the larger three-day events) are sometimes known. Experience in the show-jumping ring also comes in useful, as such events include a show-jumping element. The first phase of a one-day event is the dressage test, which forms an important part of such competitions. Many ponies and their riders find the jumping phases well within their capabilities and enjoy practising for them, but the dressage test often causes problems. In fact at this level the test is just a simple one, and should not be difficult to perform reasonably well. Devised by the Pony Club, it involves a series of movements which must be performed in order, but none of these is very advanced. The object of the dressage test is to demonstrate that the pony is well enough schooled to be able to perform simple movements smoothly and correctly in obedience to the aids, maintaining balance and impulsion both on circles and when moving straight; and that the rider is able to ride quietly and effectively, in full control of his pony and applying the aids correctly. The test consists of walking, trotting, and cantering on both reins within the test arena, which is marked out with letters to indicate where the transitions of pace and changes of direction are to be made. Only in advanced dressage tests for horses are complex movements demanded; these are beyond the scope of ponies and their riders and are not necessary for all-rounders. It is true to say, however, that a pony which is well schooled and obedient enough to perform a competent dressage test is likely to be a better all-rounder; its use of its muscles, its suppleness and obedience and balance should all help it to jump properly.

Adult three-day events are held with one phase taking place on each of the three days; the various phases of a one-day event are held in a different order, and in a scaled-down form, for both adult and junior competitions. The dressage test is performed first, followed by a modest show-jumping course; the most gruelling phase, the cross-country, is held last. In a three-day event the speed and endurance phase, of which the cross-country forms a part (it also includes work on roads and tracks, and a steeplechase course) is held on the second day, and the show-jumping phase is used as a test of the horses' fitness to jump obediently after the ordeal of the second day.

For an ambitious rider with a good all-round pony eventing presents the greatest challenge of all the competitive sports because it demands a variety of skills and is the most complete test of pony and rider. For spectators, show jumping perhaps offers the most convenient and most exciting sport to watch. But for those who are truly interested in riding, the combined-training events provide the most varied and absorbing occasions.